HEARING VOICES
listening handbook

BUCALO GIUSEPPE

ISBN: **1507707878**
ISBN-13: **978-1507707876**

CONTENTS

PROLOGUE

"How do you know but every Bird that cuts the airy way
Is an immense world of delight, closed by your senses five?"
(W. Blake)

If there is a paradox that drives our culture, it is the one that compels us to believe only what we see and that, at the same time, asks us to *prove* it exists. We must believe our eyes but only up to the moment when what we see is or may be seen by others. If we cannot record the voice that speaks to us or photograph the person who does, we should not believe our eyes, or our ears. If we do, we run the risk of being relegated to the margins of social and human reality and forced by any means to give up communicating our experience.

It should not be difficult to accept that the *reality* of this wall is the result of my perception. If I were blind I would not experience it unless I bumped into it. The sense of touch would replace my sight in a painful but concrete manner. If we were blind we would describe reality from the sounds and smells that populate it. We would not have a picture of it, we would not find sensible to perceive shapes or to think that where there is a sound there must necessarily be something (or someone) that has produced it. We wouldn't even think about it. The wall would simply not exist and no one would believe that the experience of bumping into it were real. If someone were to say that there is something like a wall, a shape, or some colours, they would soon be sectioned and their brain would be studied to understand what is wrong with its functioning.

At least this is what is happening more and more often to people who *hear voices* that cannot be recorded, that are not perceived by most of us and that come from invisible people or inanimate objects. Their ears work perfectly. They hear our voices, frightened by what they are telling us, as clearly as the voices that suggest them to shut up. Often these *voices* are more meaningful and well-advised than we are. Not always.

One of the fundamental mistakes that I see in our relationship to this experience lies in the question that we usually ask ourselves and those who hear voices. We say '*What*'s going on?', when we should ask '*Who* is speaking?'. If we hear a voice on the stairs we do not ask *what*'s going on. We realize immediately that *someone* is coming up. If we are curious, we can ask *who* it is and if we recognize the voice, we can call out and wait for them to catch up with us. OK. To understand what I mean, try to think that the friend you've heard down stairs never reaches your landing. You heard them, but they were not there. If you wonder 'Who was that?' you believe your ears. If you wonder 'What's happening to me?' you are beginning to doubt your sanity and to fear that others are doing the same. If you ask yourself 'Who', you leave the search for the meaning and the reality of that *voice* open. If you ask yourself 'What', you wipe out this experience and you look for something wrong *in* you.

I believe that no one can deny the legitimacy of both hypotheses. There is, in the present state of our knowledge, nothing that could exclude the *reality* of the voice that we have heard on the stairs, or nothing that could, on the contrary, *prove* it.

The question of whether or not to believe that there really is someone who calls us from the stairs is a relatively recent product of the idea of the world and of the mind that we have formed. It is most likely a false problem.

Human beings have always believed in the possibility of expanding the area of their perception and have looked for ways and tools to do it. Implicitly they have always believed that there are realities *outside* and *inside* of us that we cannot perceive with the senses but which are crucially important for our existence. Think of the movements of the heart and the functioning of our entire body, the rotation of the earth on its axis or the oxygen we breathe. All things that are damn *real* and *invisible* at the same time, essential both to those who believe the *voices* they hear, and those who believe that they should have their head examined.

Microscopes, telescopes, walkie-talkies ... If we had not put all the tenacity we can into believing, against all evidence and proof, that there was something else in addition to what our eyes and our ears were able to perceive, now most of what we consider obvious would be sensibly considered *delusional*.

As usual, however, the scientific revolution, after opening unexpected possibilities to our sensory capacities, has established an almost absolute perceptual dictatorship. Only that which can be *proven* is *real*. Since the *certainty* of what we perceive with the senses has been destroyed, the only *sure thing* that matters is what can be recorded and played back by the tools at our disposal.

So we happen to see crowds of spiritualists who seek *evidence* for the existence of the afterlife through the *recordings* of dead people's voices or the *photographs* of ghosts. These documents are used to *prove* on the one hand the sanity of those who speak, on the other to *demonstrate* the continuity, in the *otherworld*, of the laws of the *world*. The ultimate goal of scientific knowledge of the world is not to *understand* the nature of reality, but to keep it under *control*. In this sense, the *mind* of the spiritualists works the same way as that of the materialists. Translating the language of the *other*world to recordable and audible stimuli shows the actual substantiality of the souls, their being subjected to the same physical laws to which our bodies are subjected. *Perceiving* the souls of the dead means somehow being able to control them, to set limits to their actions, to trap them. *Spiritualism* therefore adds little to our knowledge of reality, more than anything else it tries to enlarge the domain of reason even to the immaterial worlds that affect our visible lives.

It is no coincidence that the spiritualists avoid that mass psychiatrisation which systematically touches people claiming to *hear voices*. Spiritualists are a community, they have built a theory of reference that explains what happens to them and they have specific instructions on what to do and how to behave in every situation. The *voices* that they hear are normally evoked and their nature is, for the spiritualist, clear. Given certain conditions and rituals, they *expect* to hear the voice of some dead or being that belongs to the community of the afterlife, as well as we imagine it and describe it. Once the problem of figuring out *who* is talking is overcome, the question arises on a level of mere listening (*what* is being said, to *whom* and *why*). The focus of the spiritualist is all about hearing and demonstrating to hear a *voice*. It's clear that such expectation ensures that the experience of the *voices* is lived just like any other perception of the shared reality, with the same peace of mind or emotion that a known experience can give us.

The keystone of this experience is represented by the meaningful *dialogue* that is established between *there* and *here*. Hearing voices or being a visible channel of the departed souls is a form of *relationship*; it is considered as such and is experienced as such by a community of individuals. This means that, despite every psychiatric endeavour, the spiritualist experience today is largely recognized as within the limits of the normal human belief systems. It is in fact based on a faith and hope that are common to the vast majority of human beings that inhabit the planet earth: the survival of the soul after death.

We will return to this subject. Now it is sufficient to note the fact that the scientific outlook on the world shears off a whole series of information and experiences, both good and bad, which are crucial for the development of human communities. We will never know how our lives would have been without the *dialogue* of Moses with God or the Annunciation. We can only be certain that today neither the one nor the other could avoid a psychiatric assessment and possibly hospitalization.

Yet we owe to a *Voice*, God's one, the revelation of the universal code of human behaviour; and again a *Voice* announced and accompanied the birth of a man, Jesus Christ, in whose name millions of human beings have died, have killed, have built and destroyed their lives, have judged and have been judged...

Thus, even if one day psychiatrists were able to demonstrate that there was no Angel or any god speaking to them and to show that those *voices* were the result of biochemical processes taking place in Mary's and Moses's brains, this would not change the facts and *their* reality. The fact that you can't be *certain* about something, that doesn't mean that that thing is not *true*. We can get trapped in a room whether because we were locked in, or for fear of getting out. We are trapped anyway, whether the door was kept closed or left open.

Humans, after all, do not live on *certainties* only, but above all on *truth*.

Those Christians who, nowadays, get worked up about discerning genuine vocation *from* delusion should recall the tenacity and the fate of their ancestors, who were put to death because they, with their faith, denied the established order. Monotheism, in fact, is not only a faith, but especially a vision of the world, of human beings and the relationship between them. The early Christians were persecuted for reasons similar to those that now justify hospitalization and psychiatric therapies. What they were preaching must have seemed entirely irrational, senseless and dangerous to their contemporaries. In fact each new faith, initially in particular, calls the established authority into question, at least because it doesn't recognize its sovereignty anymore and it doesn't share its laws. Let's think of how crazy the Christian imperative 'do not kill' must have appeared to the Romans. An imperative that was stronger than any law, threat or death sentence. An imperative that could disintegrate the empire that was conquered by their army and their violence. The God whom they worshiped was the only real authority they would recognize. God's laws were the only laws they complied with.

The early Christians were perfectly insane according to the official definitions that psychiatrists use to make their diagnoses. In fact, they believed in an invisible, impossible and hallucinatory reality. They were not integrated into the social and cultural context in which they lived. Their actions were in breach of the laws of civilized life and criminal laws. The justifications for their actions were delusions and fantasies, devoid of any objective evidence....

Of course, no psychiatrist would be able, today, to convince someone that Mary was only a young hysterical girl or that Moses was a schizophrenic experiencing hallucinations. However, a proper application of the psychiatric logic to their *cases* would lead to assessments of this kind, with the consequences that we know.

The Annunciation to Mary or the transmission of the commandments to Moses, are *events* that, although we cannot wipe off, we can certainly neutralize by relegating them to the realm of symbol, fantasy and imagination. If we did not do so, we would have to accept the basic truth that most of our ideas about the meaning of human existence and legitimacy of human behaviors stem from experiences that today we would call *hallucinatory*. Many of us believe, in fact, in truths that are the result of dialogues with *voices*, similar to the dialogues in which psychiatric inmates or maladjusted people in train stations around the world are engaged. They are *revealed* truths, because they are communicated by a divine, disembodied and invisible *Voice*.

The *symbolic* interpretation of these experiences serves the purpose of counteracting the influence of the voices in our material and mental life. There is no one speaking, the *voice* that we *imagine* hearing is the result of an inner *monologue* that we, in some way, produce. The *fact* of hearing voices would therefore be a *symptom* of the emergence of inner experiences: the *fact* that whole communities of individuals could give the voices credit, would only be an expression of a cultural need.

Such a hypothesis is correct and acceptable to the extent that it is not proposed as an explanation of the *scientific* and *objective* reality, overlooking that it is itself the result of profound individual and collective needs. If it is plausible to think that people *invent* the voices with which they speak to overcome loneliness, it is equally correct to think that those who try to convince us of this are actually trying to overcome the concern that their existence create in our existence. *Denying* reality to the voices is not an act of common sense or rationality: it is a psychological need. It is the result of fear and terror caused by any experience that is beyond our rational control or the control of our instruments.

Before attempting to remove the speck in the ear of those who hear *voices*, psychologists would do well to pull out the beam that is stuck in their eyes.

Denying is the rallying cry that we use with each other to keep the *voices* and those who hear them at a distance. The fact that we do so through an interpretation that is psychiatric (and, hence, we say those who hear them are nuts) or psychological (and, therefore, we say they *imagine* to hear them), does not change the substance of the matter. In both cases, we refuse to open a *dialogue* with them, stating that there is no one to talk to, or that they themselves are the result of an interior *monologue*.

We should ask ourselves why our culture has developed a system of methodical *denial* of this as well as of other human experiences. Our era, in fact, is the only one in which *hearing voices* has no chance of making sense other than the one that is imposed by others; in which *dialogue* with them is considered a symptom of a disease; in which every form of relationship is denied. This is, at least, in principle. There are also more and more situations where this perceptive cage that we have built gets demolished, the experience comes out from the solitude of inner *dialogue* and becomes collective heritage, a place for stimulating discussion, a truth-seeking tool.

These are, for example, the ecstatic gatherings in places of Marian apparitions. The Madonna's visions and messages are heard and transmitted by children or people who are humble, and once they are transcribed and circulated, they stimulate reflections, produce changes and influence our behavior.

Often it is argued that certain phenomena of collective acceptance of facts that are pathological per se, as *hearing voices* is for psychiatry, arise from the need for reassurance and from the all-human search for meaning in life. But what is it that makes us say that the need to eat is concrete and food is real, whereas the need to understand is ethereal and the voice that speaks to us is unreal? If we listed all the certainties that we have been able to find about ourselves and the world around us, if we organised them in every possible scheme, if we analysed them in all their depth, meaning and connections, in the end we would not come to anything even remotely resembling an answer as to why we are here and why we should stay here or go away. My ears allow me to hear the sounds that occur around and within me, but the fact that I can *listen* to someone doesn't depend on them. It's important that I am able to hear the car horn warning me of the danger around the bend, but it is not less practical to be able to listen to those who are in front of us in order to understand what they want from us.

Thinking that a *real* need, like the one of solving the mystery of our existence on this planet, must be answered with a certainty that is similar to a hamburger, is not a sensible and rational fact, but only the ill-fated attempt to silence questions and issues which, if posed, are going to destroy the illusory reality in which we are hiding. It happens to me sometimes, as I write, to think that I'll die, somehow, somewhere and at some time. This thought makes all the certainties that move my life useless. What's the point of writing, still? Observing traffic lights? Being careful not to offend the sensibility of people? Eating? Presenting at a conference? Paying a mortgage or building a house?... Materialists from all over the world should thank the irrational spiritualists of every age and place, if their world made of concreteness, bodies, asphalt and so on, has not yet turned into a huge real carnage, into a foolish and mad swarming, into the end of everything.

We have now acquired as a *certainty* that our *immaterial* needs are real to the extent that they can change our biochemistry and our body in an incisive and enduring way. We believe that they can even make us *see* and *hear* people who are not there, have relationships with them and do what they tell us. However, we continue to consider unreal the answers we give to them. We keep saying that there is no one speaking to us. Paradoxically, it is as if we recognized the *reality* of our need to eat and then we say that the sandwich we're swallowing does not exist. We continue, that is, to consider these responses as an expression of purely subjective reality. The *voices* that speak to us cannot be recorded, or heard by others, while our sandwich is tempting and can be tasted by everyone.

The invisibility of the experience of *hearing voices* is not sufficient on its own to demonstrate that they do not *objectively* exist, that they are independent from the person who perceives them. First of all because the existence of external *reality* is still a mystery to the extent that, strictly speaking, one could say that nothing has objective existence beyond what we can perceive. In this sense, everything we perceive would reveal itself as just a waking dream (or nightmare). Secondly because we can't exclude the possibility that there are forms of communication and modes of perception that only some of us are able to develop, but that everybody, given certain circumstances, can learn to use. This is at least what can sensibly be inferred from the universality of the experience of hearing voices in every age and culture.

We can say that *hearing voices* is a way of perceiving reality and the living beings that reside in it. As well as every other perceptual experience, it is limited and it can be misleading. We can misunderstand what we're listening to, or the *voices* can suggest things that turn out to be false, or even they may want to make fun of us. After all, these are the risks of any human communication.

The understanding of what another person is saying to us, as well as the giving credit to or obeying them, is a complex process in which the fact of hearing and understanding their words or commands, is only one of the aspects that are involved.

The fact of believing that what is being said is true derives also – and above all - from our relationship with the speaker, their role or function, from our recognition of their authority. The place where the communication takes place, the speaker's presentation and their way to disclose the issue, the information we have about them, our past experiences... have some influence too.

Generally the expression "you're lying" is used, regardless of whether there is an objective evidence of this. This is what happens, for example, to those of us who meet and fall in love with people who are hurt by previous relationships. They can't believe (and won't believe) that we are telling them the truth about our feelings. Yet they have no evidence that states the contrary. The same happens to people who have been subjected to a psychiatric assessment: their words lose their meaning and credibility regardless of the evidence that they give. Their speech by definition is wrong, false and senseless. This goes to the extremes of considering every complaint of physical or sexual abuse suffered by them *delusional* or even just *symbolic* (and therefore unreal). The word of a psychiatrised person is not admitted in court, he often doesn't have the chance to attend, intervene, defend their reasons if interrogated, based on a psychiatric report.

The examples could go on forever. Analyzing our daily interactions and the way we listen to and give credit to others, we could dissect other variables that cause us to believe what we are told, to obey an order or to take someone's advice. These examples are useful as they lead us to try and think of the phenomenon of *hearing voices* as a *possible* experience of communication.

One of the things that unsettle us most in accepting the *reality* of the voices is in fact the idea that they can influence the behaviours of the listener to the point of making him commit acts that are harmful for themselves and others. I am not referring only to the fact that we believe they may *command* people to kill themselves or someone else, but also to the simple fact that they may advise them and force them to quit their jobs, set fire to their savings on the streets, destroy their home furniture, press charges and speak out against relatives and friends, etc.

The hypothesis at first glance seems *reasonable*, supported by news reports and eyewitness accounts of people who claim to have acted in obedience to one or more *voices*, but in fact it only hides our fear to face the reality of us being human and, therefore, influenced and at the mercy of a human and material world on which often we have no control.

Some examples. If I were now to command you, peremptorily, to leave the house and lie under a pouring rain waiting for a sign from God, probably the majority of you would not do it. But if I were a sub-officer in the Italian army and you were conscripts, you would feel you had no other choice but to get up quickly and obey the order, however absurd it may seem to you. Even though in both cases I used the same words, in only one case I have been obeyed. We obey an order when we recognize authority in those who issue it or when we are threatened by them, irrespective of the meaningfulness of the order.

There is virtually no difference in shooting other human beings under the orders of a superior officer or the voice of Satan. There is not for those who fall under our shots, there is not for the moral and human responsibility that we take, and there is not for the mechanisms that lead us to obey that order. People do not obey the *voices* they hear regardless: they obey them if they recognize their authority, they fear their reactions, they agree with their analyses, they want them to stop talking ... People behave like they usually do when they become quiet in libraries, when they answer questions asked by a judge, when they give up eating meat, when they wear Mum's woollen sweater...

The *voices* have authority and power for at least two reasons:

• because they are *disembodied*;
• because they make *sense*.

There is nothing closer to a person than the *voice* he/she hears. Obviously it knows the person better than anyone else and is able to soothe the person's wounds or rub salt in them. Much of their authority and their influence stems from the fact that they seem to have access to our most intimate secrets, to be aware of our most hidden thoughts, to know our weaknesses.

The *voices* always know what words to use to be heard by us. We do not have any chance to remain indifferent, because they always talk *about* us in the most visceral, radical and inescapable way. What they have to say is all the most important or disturbing stuff we can expect to hear from another human being. There isn't any place where they can't reach us. The sound of their words is not subject to the limitations of the matter: there is no door, wall, sound that can prevent us to *hear them*. Somehow we hear these *voices* with our whole body, as if we have become a huge living ear, an eardrum which vibrates in unison with them.

The *voices* know us perhaps better than we know ourselves. Their advice always makes *sense* even when they push us to expose ourselves and risk our social and material life. Often the usual *reasons* for our uncritical acceptance of reality cannot compete with the *irrational* urge to get to the bottom of things.

There is nothing that we can think or do that is not already in our human potential. The advice that we follow, in some way, is already written in us or in our history. The *voices* think on our behalf. They say the things we can't say. They choose for us. They convince us of the need to revolutionize our existence and they show us the way to do it. I don't think there is anything that they can convince us of, that we are not already convinced of ourselves. This is also when we need to hide behind their *coercion* in order not to take responsibility to understand what we did or what happened.

The example of the murderer of John Lennon is emblematic of the prejudice and the reality of our relationship with the authority and power of the *voices*. The Court that judged him *reasonably* requested a psychiatric assessment to determine whether the act of the murderer had been caused by some kind of psychiatric illness. In particular, the murderer had declared that he had acted under the influence, the advice or the order of demonic voices that had convinced him of the *betrayal* by Lennon of the purpose of social transformation. This was sufficient for the newspapers and the public to conclude that the murder of the singer was just another murderous rampage of a madman. A senseless, unmotivated, irrational act. Lennon was dead because of this mental disorder and not by free choice of someone. A senseless death itself.

This way of thinking that seemed to the Court, as well as it usually seems to us, *well-advised*, actually throws the death of a man and the life of his murderer into nothingness. It doesn't allow to understand and, even worse, it creates a myth of *hearing voices* that affirms the *presumption* of dangerousness of this experience. The psychiatric assessment, in acquitting the person from the responsibility of choosing to kill, imputes liability of the murder to the *voices*, turning the thousands of people who hear them into potential murderers to be afraid of, and into scared beings themselves, besieged between the fear of losing control and the fear of being caught. It must be said that it is the secrecy in which we force those who hear *voices*, the factor that decisively influence their ability to control, understand and make the most of this experience. I think we are all equally responsible for the failure of this *dialogue* and the tragic consequences that *sometimes* come with it. Had it been possible for Lennon's murderer to talk and compare his *reasons* and the reasons of his *voices*, with our own or those of Lennon, probably this conflict could have been resolved in a less iniquitous way. We will come back to these collective responsibilities.

Now it must be remembered that the murderer refused to submit himself to the assessment and asked to be judged for what he had done. In particular, in an interview, while reviewing the positions that led him to act, he stated clearly he did not consider the demons or the *voices* responsible for what he had done. He was *consciously* convinced that the allegations, analyses and ideas of the voices were correct, as well as the order to punish the traitor. Giving responsibility for what he had done to the suggestions he had received, is as equally grotesque as to say that the blame for the suicide of a couple of young lovers can be given to a work of art and passion like Shakespeare's Romeo and Juliet, found on the victims' bedside table. This way of thinking is perhaps more irrational than the action it intends to deny: it comes from the personal and social need to avoid seeing, understanding, dialoguing, hearing.

The murderer in this interview was in my opinion very clear in describing the issue of responsibility with regards to the act he had committed. He said that the *voices* had always been with him, they had accompanied him for months without a break, not even for a minute. This was up to the moment before he pulled the trigger. When he shot John Lennon everything, in and around him, was completely silent. He was the one who pulled the trigger and at that time he was *alone*.

Often these *voices* do not have a body; they appear as disembodied and invisible entities.

They are pure sound, not produced by the human larynx. What they provoke in our fragile materiality is not dissimilar to what Adam and Eve experienced in the presence of the voice of god after eating the apple. Being naked, alone and at the mercy of an invisible but inexorable entity and plan.

Those who speak to us cannot be seen, arrested, silenced. They do not have a body that we can trap behind a door. They do not have an identity that we can recognize and despise. In our unconscious, the invisible being is the origin of all things, the creator and at the same time, the destroyer of reality.

The invisible inhabits the places where our thoughts and our secrets lie. There is nothing you can hide away from it. While we keep the bodies and minds of other *material* people at a distance, there is nothing we can do against its invasion. It can penetrate every cell in our bodies and take possession of it, think our thoughts and anticipate our decisions.

The power that we confer to the *voices* is not unlike the one we imagine it is possessed by invisible (whether material or fantastic) entities that affect our lives. We seriously believe that those who have no body indeed have access to the knowledge of the laws that govern the life and the material existence of us all. Not only that, but we also believe that they can influence and determine what happens to us.

After all, mankind has always believed in these immaterial presences that determine human events. It has always believed that they are *willing* and *able* to change the reality in which we live. Angels, goblins, demons, gods ... they have often decided about men and their destiny. This, if possible, makes it even more complex to establish some kind of reciprocal and equally collaborative relationship with the *voices*. There is, in fact, an ontological difference between the *voices* and us. While sharing the same *reality*, we have and act different existences and possibilities. If it is true that we *can't* see and hear the thoughts of other human beings, it is also true that the *voices*, in general, are not allowed to act on matter except through us. Those who hear *voices* and believe to be dependent on them, in my opinion, should consider whether, and to what extent, the *voices* they hear *need* them instead.

Augusto, for example, often wanders near the hospital. He tells me that somewhere in the wall he sees / hears an old man who speaks to him and predicts the future. He, as a good inhabitant of our reasonable world, always checks any information he receives. Until now, the old man was never wrong.

Augusto is standing there listening to him because, he says, he knows that the old man needs him. Without Augusto the old man would not exist. He would be invisible, pushed here and there by unsuspecting people who are deaf to his calls. Even now he doesn't have an easy life. Men have gradually equipped themselves for centuries to seal all doors that allow the old man to enter into the spectrum of our visual, auditory, tactile or olfactory perception. Augusto has already been psychiatrised and they are looking for him again. He fights not only for his freedom and his lucidity, but also for the old man who is very little danger to his mental and physical integrity, as compared to the poisons that they inject into his veins or compared to the nurses in a psychiatric ward.

The urgency of action is not due to the need to *take care of* Augusto. What moves them all is the need to put an end to the matter he takes up with the social and family order in which he is included. If he follows the *orders* of the old man, he will no longer be available to follow the social order. So he won't shower, he won't work, he will sleep on the ground or at the train stations, he will beg, etc. That is to say he will behave like all the saints and mystics who have lived on our planet over the millennia.

I have often heard *reasonable* people say that Augusto may do what he likes, provided he behaves like a civilized person. He may continue to *hear* the old man, but he should not neglect his family, work, personal hygiene, sleep... He should consider as a *fantasy* something that is a true *reality* for him. Experience shows that this is not possible.

The experience of *hearing voices*, often but not always, completely overturns our identity. Not much is left of us, our expectations and our social existence after being *touched*. Often what happens is a *rebirth*, we are enlightened by the light of a revelation that finally gives meaning to our presence in the world. The fact that others around us refuse to recognize our new life, is an integral part of the revelation and our surrender to it. Those who are on the path of truth know that they must expect a persecution that is more cruel and senseless the more their faith is genuine.

Besides, even the Gospels are sprinkled with notations of this nature. For example, in the Gospel of Matthew where Jesus says, "*Whoever loves father or mother more than me is not worthy of me, and whoever loves son or daughter more than me is not worthy of me, and whoever does not take his cross and follow me is not worthy of me. Whoever finds his life will lose it, and whoever loses his life for my sake shall find it*". Or again: "*Do not think that I have come to bring peace to the earth. I have not come to bring peace, but a sword. For I have come to set a man against his father, and a daughter against her mother, and a daughter-in-law against her mother-in-law. And a person's enemies will be those of his own household.*"

There is no doubt that the enemies of our every transformation can be sought between the people who are closest. In fact, they build their identity based on ours. Fathers may be, for example, only if we are children. The fact that we can change is in itself an unacceptable *betrayal* of the family/mental order in which we live. However, it is inevitable and necessary, especially when we are *called*, like the Disciples of Christ who gave everything up to follow him.

To follow ourselves and our *inner guidance* we often have to break up with everything and everyone. This is the inevitable corollary of our decision to focus on *dialogue* and inner *search* as a royal road to the understanding of ourselves and the world. This initial moment of closure and even dramatic break, is temporary and has the function to conclude a phase of our existence, in the same way as stripping himself naked in the streets was necessary to Francis in order for him to get rid of his previous identity and his links with the established order, symbolically and practically.

If this is allowed, the next step is to build a heated *dialogue* with the *vo(i)c(e)ation* that guides us to change our lives and those of others. We will see further examples of how such a dialogue can bring good results.

For now, let us ask ourselves how a *voice* can determine transformations that are so radical in human beings. If language usually helps building a mental and social order inside and outside of us, it can also destroy it. This is what *voices* often do: they overthrow the order of reality.

This is even *true*r as we reflect on the fact that all the doctrines, techniques and philosophies that promote an overcoming of our vision of the world and the search for a new mental and cosmic order, agree on the need to stop the *internal dialogue* as an essential prerequisite for making every change *possible*. This indicates that language has a much deeper function than just the communicative or evocative ability. This means that it not only allows us to communicate *with* humans and *about* reality, but somehow it makes their existence *possible*. As Don Juan tells Castaneda: "*When you reach the silence, everything is possible.*" (C. CASTANEDA 1992, p. 146).

Everything is possible because, when carefully viewed, the thing that holds together the *meaning* of what we call *reality* seems to be our constant inner dialogue in which we name and define things according to the conventional order that we have established for ourselves. Without realizing it, except in certain states of consciousness, we constantly define (and create) *reality*. This is a chair, this is a finger, this is me, this is a table, this is a hand, and so on. The inner dialogue immediately translates perceptions into something real and known. It therefore constructs a way of recognizing what needs to be considered as such.

If we take a look at the way we educate our children to perceive and acknowledge *reality*, we clearly see the importance of our constant endeavour of suggesting to them, through language, the name of all things, actions, emotions and behaviour. We do with them what the *voices* often do with us: we try to educate their perception to enable them to perceive reality as we think it should be. Without the mediation of language, no child can be integrated in a natural and spontaneous way in this reality. It is a fact that perceptual skills in children are broader and less organized than those of adults. Although this is often considered a limitation to be overcome with education, it is actually a distinct possibility that we have, to be able to see and feel reality more fully. It is no coincidence that the philosophies which seek inner transformation argue that we must return to be as *pure* as children. The purity to which they refer is, in my view, the perceptive one. The one that allows them to see their true face and reality just as it is, without the mediation of consciousness or language.

If children are convinced that the fire burns, this happens because of the evidence of this experience as well as for the fact that we repeat to them that such event is called fire and such experience of intense pain is named burn. Our words mean that children learn to perceive fire as fire, to recognize the mechanisms, methods, times and places in which one can sensibly expect it to spread. They do not learn to perceive the fire; they learn to limit this definition to a clear set of perceptions.

So if they see a flame suddenly suspended in the air, and a *voice* speaks to them, they won't believe their eyes or ears. They will do what we all do in the face of experiences that terrify us: they will repeat to themselves or out loud 'There isn't any fire and no one is speaking to me', believing that this will get rid of the flame and the voice.

What does this magical belief come from if not from the fact that we, somehow, know that it is our inner dialogue, our faith, our belief in what is *real* that influence or determine what we perceive? We know that if we cease to believe that we see something there before us, it will disappear into thin air. This knowledge is, in my opinion, a childhood reminiscence of the process through which the *voice* of adults educated, modified, canceled and replaced our perceptions.

Often those who hear *voices*, at least in the early stages, use this technique to cope with this experience and to try not to go crazy. Manuela, for example, used to go to the bathroom, open the taps and loudly describe everything she was doing. This strategy worked for her. Manuela would thus manage to limit her perceptual capacities, anchoring them again to the shared reality. In describing what she was doing as she was doing it or what was around her, she would anchor her body, her senses and her mind in that patch of *reality* in which she had always lived. To the *voice* that was speaking to her, she would oppose her own *voice*, to the *reality* that it was imposing to her, she contrasted the shared *reality*.

It must be said that such strategies, although widespread, are often ineffective or even dangerous. Firstly, they require an enormous expenditure of energy. Secondly, their management is complicated by the fact that they can't be acted except in situations of sound insulation and relational isolation. Using such techniques in public places, at home, in the street and, in any case, in the presence of others, easily exposes us to the risk of judgment by others and psychiatric hospitalizations. It is to be borne in mind, in fact, that only in some cases it is possible to face the *voices* on a mental and, therefore, inner plane. In most cases if we use this denial technique, an escalation of sound is established, so you need to raise your voice and increase the speed of descriptions in order to keep up with the *voices*. It is clear that this is possible only in a limited number of situations and occasions. Too few to be able to cope with an experience that, in general, happens daily in our lives, at times and in places that are quite diverse.

This example should be considered, therefore, not so much as a guide to listening to the *voices*, but as a statement of the meaning and power of language in relation to the construction of reality.

Antonio has been in constant relationship with St. Philip for more than twenty years. The saint has guided his choices and has been close to him in every difficult moment of his existence. It could be argued that Antonio has not made any decision without first consulting and listening to the advice of the saint. Indeed, he has always followed his advice, even when he did not fully understand it.

It's impossible to describe Antonio's human and social history without describing his relationship with the saint. He is not a mere fantasy, at the very least because his words have determined certain choices and material transformations in the life of Antonio and his family; with him and his advice we have to deal, regardless of whether or not we believe in his existence.

The authority of St. Philip was built over the years through a material check of meaningfulness and accuracy of the advice received. He has, so to speak, won Antonio's obedience and respect, behaving and acting like one would expect from a saint.

The identity of a *voice* is revealed through the actions it does and the congruence of what it says. That's what convinces us. After all, the search for facts that prove the existence and nature of the invisible is part of the history of our relationship with it. So the saints are also identified for their miracles and Christ is resurrected because we are able to touch the wounds on his rib cage. Thomas, if you will, represents the universal need to touch the substantiality and materiality of the divine. Only this way we are enabled to believe completely and with passion.

The *voices* often assume power and authority on us just for their ability, that seems *supernatural*, to predict events and judge people. This ability is not *claimed*, it is *proven to be true* by thousands of big and small examples that concern our daily lives. These *proofs* that each *voice* provides to those who hear them are used to seal the pact between the voices and the humans. Without miracles of this nature there is no *dialogue* between us, only annoying noises or obsessive phrases that drive us crazy.

Confucius said that the easiest way out is through the door, but no one seems to use it. Similarly, to the experience of hearing *voices* the most sensible response would seem to be asking "*Who* are you?", but this is already considered a symptom of mental illness.

Many of the people who hear *voices* have never answered them. How would you feel if you were speaking to someone and they ignored you? Surely this would annoy you. The nonverbal message that you'd come across would be like "I do not care what you have to say. To me you do not exist. Why don't you piss off?!" The noxious idea that we've got is that by pretending we don't hear them, the *voices* will suddenly disappear. In fact the only result we often obtain is to trigger in them a mechanism of accusation and criticism against us. We could argue that our attention is a matter of survival for the *voices*. If we disinvest part of our energy from our perception, we endanger their existence. Once again I stress that those who hear *voices* should understand clearly that the *voices* often need them more than they need the *voices*.

But let's hear how this works from the words of those who tried to ignore the *voices*:

In the end I decided to ignore the voices and I asked them to leave me alone. In my ignorance I chose the wrong way to tackle the problem. You can't put aside anything that exists within yourself and that manifests so intensely. Moreover, this would have led to the fact that the voices would have lost their right to exist for the lack of attention and energy; of course this was not what they wanted. Until then, the voices had been friendly and polite, but they changed in the opposite direction, they said all sorts of oddities and ridiculed the things that were important to me. It was a no-holds-barred civil war, but I was determined to win and I continued to ignore everything. And I managed to do it by keeping busy throughout the day. At that time I did a lot of crossword puzzles, my house had never been so clean, and the garden had never been so well looked after. The result was that life became calmer, but in a forced way. I could hardly relax. (Cited in M.A.J. ROMME and A.D.M.A.C. ESCHER 1988)

Ignoring them or trying to keep the brain and ears engaged are just two of the strategies that we normally use to try to wipe the *voices* off. Surely they are the most natural and instinctive strategies. In addition to these, a central role, by diffusion, is also played by the use of prescribed or self-prescribed chemicals. We take these substances, whether legal (psychotropic medications, alcohol) or illegal (illicit drugs), in order to limit the expansion of our consciousness and our perception. The goal is to eliminate or at least mitigate the devastating effect that the *voices* have on our personal and social safety.

Once again, all our attention is focused on ourselves, nothing is done in terms of trying to face and silence the voices. We do not act on the transmitter, we kick the receiver. The only concrete things on which we can act are, after all, the senses and the brain of the listener. In fact we can't see a deep throat that speaks, nor can we identify a body, let alone believe that it exists somehow or somewhere.

Antonio, for example, takes psychiatric medications. The experience of living under the benevolent gaze of St. Philip, although it doesn't create any personal problem for him, provokes a deep crisis in the social and family order into which he is integrated. St. Philip makes himself *heard* whenever Antonio has a problem or is faced with a choice. In those moments he is *unwell*. He means that he doesn't know what to do and he is anxious about his decision. In these moments the *voice* of St. Philip accompanies him, comforts him and advises him. He is not unwell because of this intrusion. On the contrary he considers it a necessary *cure* to break the deadlock to which he has come.

The question then moves to another level. Accepting the advice of St. Philip basically results in rejecting anyone's arguments and advice. In other words, Antonio refuses to listen to his wife or relatives with regards to what should be done, proving, in their eyes, to be unreasonable. Not only that; his behaviour while he listens to the advice of the saint, is indecipherable for everybody. He holds a dialogue with a person that others do not see, he laughs at jokes they do not hear, he pauses to listen to inaudible words. It is hard to live next to someone who has a perception of the world which is different from ours: even if we seem to be in the same room we are in fact on two different planets. It is more or less the same distance that there is between me writing and my wife with her Walkman on the couch listening to music. It can be very embarrassing, disturbing and incomprehensible, to see her move on the wave of a music that I can't hear... as well as it can be a sight of a heavenly sweetness.

Antonio often has that typical ecstatic expression of someone who seems to be *touched* by God. That same expression others may call *stupor* and consider it a symptom of some mental illness. Whatever judgment we can give on what is happening to him (or on *who* speaks to him) it should always be clear that the things we see are *in* our heads and not in Antonio's.

If we think he's unwell because he spends entire nights going up and down to talk to the Saint, we must understand that we are the ones who are in crisis because he does not seem to see us anymore, or hear our words anymore. He lives as it were in a dimension on which we no longer have any influence; his mind escapes dramatically the influence our words or our feelings can exert on him. This scares us because we feel we don't have control anymore over him and over his actions, as well as it is impossible for us to predict his behaviour.

If we go deep into the matter, the idea that the *voices* can get people to do things they *normally* would not do is a projection of the fact that our *voice* seems to have lost this same power over them. We are the ones who, having lost control over the other, are terrified that he could use his *new* freedom against us or against himself. This is the mechanism that is normally triggered in us when we try to explain inconsistencies or non-shared choices of people we think we know: *something* or *someone* has forced them to act that way. We can't accept the idea that they might have *chosen* to be different from what we think of them.

There is not any *sensible* reason that can lead us to say that the words that are spoken by *invisible* people, or the relationships with them, are more or less harmful to those who entertain them, than the tangible relations that we have with visible people. Risk, pain, anxiety as well as joy, wonder, serenity, are implicit possibilities in every inter-human relationship. No one can argue with certainty that listening to the words of their parents is more sensible, or gives better results than listening to the advice of a saint, and vice versa. The effect and the nature of a relationship can be assessed only in hindsight, and often our evaluation of an experience can change over time, even drastically. What we now describe as the most beautiful time of our earthly existence, tomorrow could sensibly seem the darkest moment, the love of someone we are experiencing today, tomorrow could be the most fierce and limitless hatred. This is not inconsistency in our logic, but emotional transformations that are part of us and are themselves our raison d'être.

In order to understand the experience of *hearing voices* we do not need to bother creating a science or discipline ad hoc. We should simply use the knowledge, and, above all, the *experience* that we have developed over the centuries and are part of our genetic communication baggage.

We are in front of *people* (even though they are special) speaking with other (also special) people. What they bring to life is only an inter-human *dialogue*, nothing more or less than what commonly captivates us or turns upside down the daily lives of each of us. Accepting that this *dialogue* exists and facing the contents and the choices that flow from it, does not necessarily address the countless issues and tangles that these interactions brings into our orderly reality: it only puts us in a condition to address them with sensitivity, intelligence, respect and willpower.

This book is a *guide* for those who have never heard *voices*. It's the guide that was found by those who hear them, and who, too often, can't (or are not allowed to) get it across to our ears or our heart.

MONOLOGUE

"Jimmy McKenzie was a bloody pest at the mental hospital because he went around shouting at his voices. We could only hear one end of the conversation, but the other end could be inferred in general terms at least from; 'Away tae fuck, ye filthy bastards. . .'

It was decided at one and the same time to alleviate his distress and ours, by giving him the benefit of a leucotomy. An improvement in his condition was noted.

After the operation he went around no longer shouting abuse at his voices but, 'What's that? Say that again! Speak up ye buggers, I cannae hear ye!'

(R.D.LAING)

The criticism to the psychiatric approach to voices is a primary requirement for anyone who hopes to have a dialogue or to establish some relationship with them (and / or with the people who hear them). We have already said that the hypothesis of an organic brain imbalance as the basis and cause of these perceptions is plausible. But the fact that a hypothesis is *plausible* does not necessarily mean that it is *true*. On the contrary, I am led to believe that the biochemical changes that *certainly* accompany the experience of *hearing voices* are of the same nature and have the same function as the biochemical changes that accompany the experience of hearing the birds chirping in the courtyard. The biochemical changes that are happening in my brain right now, allow me to feel and create the sound of the birds. Probably nothing like that exists out there. It is me who translates invisible and inaudible stimuli into sound. Moreover, in this perceptual experience, I am alone anyway. I'll never know if my wife, who is busy next to me, is hearing the *same* chirping. I'm probably the only one who hears *that* song and *that* rustle of leaves in the wind.

I believe it doesn't make sense to think that the real and observable biochemical changes that occur in our brain when we hear someone's voice can be considered *healthy* or *ill* depending on our opinion about the existence or nonexistence of the speaker. Just to be scientistic by any means, we could say that our brain *hears* in the same way someone who speaks, whether he is visible or not. The question is, if anything, understanding who he is, what he wants, what he says, and, at times, how to make him stop talking.

Psychiatry has always considered its assumptions as if they were facts. It regards normality as an objective, scientific, biological fact. Human behaviours are not, for psychiatry, the effect brought about by our experiences, but rather the result of the structure of our brain as we have inherited it from our parents. For this reason, the experience of *hearing voices* can be treated like appendicitis and *cured* through a surgical, chemical, or electrical invasion of the brain.

But can one sensibly say that our choices, our tastes or our ideas are expressions or symptoms of an *illness*? And whatever kind of illness is the one that identifies with our way of being and living, with our bodies and with our senses? Can one sensibly say that those who express an opinion or a choice that we don't agree with are *ill* and, therefore, unaware of what they are saying or doing? And have all those who have for years resisted their lobotomy, their life imprisonment in mental hospitals, their electroshock not been considered affected by this *illness*? And above all, how can one say that people are suffering from an *illness* the main symptom of which is their rejection of being *ill*?

Lobotomy, insulin shock, electroshock, psycho-pharmaceutical drugs... each of these *treatments*, tested on hundreds of thousands of human beings, mostly against their will, have produced observable and demonstrable physical damage in their perfectly healthy brains. The aim of psychiatry does not seem as much to re-establish a balance in the brain function of its *im*patients, but rather to monitor and modify their behavior and their way of thinking because these are considered intolerable or unacceptable. In other words, psychiatry is not an answer to a medical problem, but to certain needs that, depending on the times, can be ethical, political, social, domestic, moral, religious...

How else can one explain the fact that *sexual delusion*, *masturbation*, *homosexuality* were for decades considered to be symptoms of, or veritable mental illness? If one continues to consider psychiatry a medical science, one cannot in any way explain how these *symptoms* and *illnesses* have become part of normality and even, in the case of homosexuality, characterise a legally protected status in many countries in the world.

The so-called *mental illnesses* are not illnesses of the brain, are *ways* to use one's body and mind in ways that are socially unacceptable in a given period and in a given human community. The fact that there are still cultures nowadays that value hearing voices as a *gift* is mirrored by the concept of *mental illness* that we use in order to define the same experience. The idea that anyone who hears voices is *ill* is a *cultural* product and not a scientific truth, as much as the idea that he was *chosen* by God.

The fact that this experience, like all human experiences, has a biochemical substrate does not allow us to call it an *illness*, to the same degree that we do not define *symptoms* of an illness the biochemical changes that allow our bodies to participate to our falling in love or that give us goose bumps when we hear a piece of music.

Similarly, the fact that this experience is universal doesn't allow us to generalize our 'scientific' point of view, claiming that this shows that it is an *illness* that is not influenced by social, economic or cultural factors. As above, this way of thinking should be applied to a range of human experiences which, in fact, are believed to be purely human: the attachment of parents to their children; falling in love; sex... These experiences are universally regarded as *symptoms* of proper social and biological functioning. This does not allow us to say that they are therefore experiences which are organic in origin, and least of all, *pathological*.

It is not clear after all, the principle according to which *scientific* opinions should be regarded as *necessarily* true, and extended to ex/pound all human experience. It is not clear, for example, according to what principle the Voice asking Abraham to sacrifice his son Isaac, should be considered a hallucination and adduced as a proof of the existence of a *mental illness*, and not show instead that all the forcedly psychiatrised people, nowadays diagnosed as schizophrenics, are actually just channels of god's will or the battlefield for the eternal struggle between the forces of good and evil.

The fact that specific biochemical processes step in to make it possible to *hear voices*, even when they are proven, do not demonstrate that this experience is an illness. Among other things, these changes do not appear related to any other disturbance in the functioning of our body. Heart disease, respiratory disease or diseases which damage any other organ in our body, have inevitable repercussions on the general functioning of our system. The so-called *mental illnesses* rather seem to have only influence on our behaviour, thoughts, and the way we relate to the world. There is no factual difference between what we call, in some occasions, *mental illnesses* and what we consider in other instances points of view, philosophical musings, identity, character... What makes someone's idea a *delusion* is the fact that it is not recognized by others. The fact that it is right or wrong, true or false, correct or flawed, does not affect the psychiatric judgment; what is needed, in order to be able to define an idea *ill*, is its subjective nature. Collective ideas, even the most terrifying and disturbing, are analyzed as an expression of human reason and intellect, even if they are wrong or immoral they are recognized as *reasonable*.

In fact, the concept of illness, which has (and should have) a well-defined range of use, is now utilised extensively; this is not justified by *scientific* needs, but it is motivated by the necessity to find philosophies that rationalise on one hand our inability to understand what happens to us, on the other hand the actions we put in place to silence and deny our and others' experiences.

The imperative that nowadays seems to move us is to not *listen* to what people and / or *voices* say. In order to do so, it wasn't and it isn't enough to consider them mere unreal fantasies, one must intervene invasively in the body, in the brain and in the existence of people to prevent them from perceiving them and disclosing their existence to others. Psychiatry has, in this case as well as in other cases, the function of covering ideologically this activity of denial and repression of the human experience. That is, it helps by transforming some acts, otherwise experienced as violent and unjust, into therapeutic techniques and strategies. When one calls someone 'mentally ill', T. SZSAZ mentions, one does not say anything about who that someone is or what that someone is going through, one only authorizes those who are close to that someone to limit his/her personal freedom of movement and choice. That which in any other situation would be considered a criminal offense becomes, through the use of psychiatric terminology, a scientific and therapeutic act.

The political use that was (and is) made of psychiatry in some authoritarian regimes, is not, as it is commonly believed, a degeneration due to volitions which are external to psychiatry itself. It is rather the most crudely and explicitly concrete realization of it. It happens what happened in mental asylums all around the world: free to act without any moral, ethical or legal limitation, psychiatrists have designed, built and operated large concentration camps with the purpose of punishing, monitoring and forcing people to change their minds as they, in one way or another, would transgress the written and unwritten laws on which our civil society is grounded.

The explicit aim of psychiatry seems to be that of transforming people, by taking into account not their personal intentions and will, but the needs of those around them. In this sense, I think we can say that there is no *use* of psychiatry that is not in itself an *abuse*.

In the prologue I talked about a *perceptual dictatorship* being imposed on our senses and our mind by the scientific view of reality. I used the word *dictatorship* meaning the fact that it is not underpinned as much, or just, by the free informed consent of each of us, but rather by a range of mystifying, coercive and threatening tools. We perceive the world in certain ways, not only because we *can* do it, but also because we *have to*.

Each of us knows that the emergence of feelings and perceptions, which are not in line with the common ways of feeling, exposes one to the psychiatric judgment and intervention. This judgment precludes the person any chance to communicate their experiences, to express their will, to live in the everyday reality. His thoughts, his ideas, his behaviour cease to be what they are, they become just the *symptoms* of an illness, *things* that can be manipulated, modified, controlled...

Psychiatric *cure* consists of making some people stop thinking about (or even just communicating) their subjective experiences. These will be well *balanced* or *healed* only when they will stop saying they believe what happens to them and they will agree with the point of view of their *therapists*. Those who do not conform to this psychiatric expectation begin an ordeal of internment and *treatment* that precludes, in actual fact, any possibility of existence. Those who conform to it cease to be (and to claim being) a person.

Once you are taken by the psychiatric spiral, there aren't many choices ahead: either you yield and accept the psychiatric judgment, agreeing to live a sheltered and subordinate life; or you resist and you gradually see your home, your friends, your job, your driver's license vanish... The psychiatric intervention does not face any problem: it just makes it disappear. Through this trick, every year, thousands of individuals disappear from the face of the earth, often just guilty of *lese reality*. They are judged by a court that considers their defense as an integral part of the offense. Any citizen, even if accused of the most unacceptable act of wickedness, has the right to defence. A psychiatric patient is instead interned and punished, considered dangerous and treated, just because he defends his point of view.

We have no evidence to suggest that *hearing voices* is an illness: the only certain thing is that the Voices have always spoken to men. The only difference between cultures, eras, and individuals, is in the kind of *dialogue* that they have established with them and in the kind of *listening* to them.

Our age has somehow chosen the path of denial of that relationship, silencing people and trying to prevent their *dialogue* with the voices.

But it hasn't always been so. It's a fact that this experience has been universally used in different cultures and eras, as a key element of mystical practices, magical rituals and cultural activities. The *voices* have driven entire communities, and have facilitated their adaptation to a hostile environment and their material, psychological and social survival. The experiences and suggestions of the *voices* for centuries have allowed men to reflect and untangle the knots of their knowledge of the world and of the reality of their existence. They took part in key decisions with which humans have organized themselves and have taken root on this planet. Often this reality is debased by representing the *dialogue* with the voices as an element of folklore belonging to certain primitive tribal cultures or to the mystic lives of some saints. The fact that the *dialogue* with them has contributed to the building of this culture of ours that is now trying to get rid of them is not taken into account, with the same blindness with which we try to deny our *roots* when we are ashamed of them.

The metaphor of the expulsion of Adam and Eve from Eden is very apt to describe this situation. They lived in a state of communion with creation, driven by the will and *word* of God. The Eden is not a physical place but a state of mind and body for which there is no *consciousness* or *responsibility*: Adam and Eve didn't have to choose, they lived and grew with the same happy unconsciousness in which trees grow. Lacking awareness, they were free from pain and suffering. They did not possess / know anything, not even their body. They were not simply disembodied; they were at one with, matter and spirit of the universe. There was nothing in them that reminded *consciousness* as we experience it. They flowed with water from the river or wandered with the clouds in the sky, the one mind dwelt in every living and non-living thing. Something similar to the experience that we have all been exposed to in the womb. No coincidence that we define our desire to re-enter it as a metaphor of Paradise. In the amniotic fluid we are one with the heartbeat of our mother, with the blood that is pumped into circulation, with the movements of her breathing... we have no more consciousness of ourselves than the heart has of itself or of rhythmically beating our intrauterine time.

I think this is the moment in which the sound and the human *voice* becomes part of us, of our cells, of our genetic heritage. In our unconscious intrauterine life there is no way to make a separation between ourselves, the stimuli we receive and our responses: we are all one and the same. We do not *perceive* the voices and sounds; we *are* those voices and sounds. Somehow this experience contributes to the construction of our body and our mind and stays as a part of them. We are sound, in addition to being matter. For this reason, sound can change matter and the human mind. Think of the biochemical reactions that are elicited in us by a love poem or an insult. Think of the altered state of consciousness in which we enter via the obsessive rhythm of tribal music. Think of the freeze response that comes from the fear of a verbal threat. How many times have we felt stunned and motionless, heart in our throat, sweating in response to the words of a superior? Nobody has injected substances in our body, has held us down or turned the air conditioner off, and yet our bodies react to those *words* as if something of that sort had happened.

In some way and at some level, sound is something primordial imprinted in our body, as well as in our spirit. Language, in this sense, can be considered a system of sounds to which is given a conventional meaning and that is recognized by a group. This system is more than just a simple social construct: it in fact uses the primordial matter from which we are made.

When we hear someone talking, his *voice*, as well as being a set of meaningful sounds, is a message that, in some way, activates our cells and the genetic memory that is kept in them. So it happens that the *voice* of God on the way to Damascus can forever change the life of Paul, as well as the OM chanted by Allen GINSBERG stopped the police charging the crowd in the seventies.

The *voices*, as well as being sounds, are human beings' expressions. Relationships with ourselves, with others and with the world are built on these sounds. If we talked for days about witches and magic, we would find immediately compelling elements and perceptual data on the presence and journey of invisible entities in our lives. Often we dismiss it all as the result of suggestion. This may be true, but the power of language is not just that. More than influencing, our discussions, as they evolve, shift our attention and alter our perception of reality, and break the unconscious control that we exercise over our senses. In a nutshell we begin to see and feel things which before we didn't pay any attention to. These facts, which we now call magic, were already present: we only become capable of perceiving them. In order to get rid of them we use the same strategy: we distract ourselves, we talk about something else, we divert our attention from searching signs and we invest again in the shared reality. In all of this language reigns supreme.

But let's go back to Heaven for a moment. We have left Adam and Eve in the amniotic primordial fluid, happy and unconscious. As we all know, they will lose this privilege because of their disobedience to God's prohibition to eat the apple from the Tree of Knowledge of Good and Evil. This act of pride and rebellion, suggested by the *voice* of the serpent, is considered the beginning of the fall of man into earthly hell, the primary cause of the suffering of mankind. This story is told to all the Catholic children of the world, as an example of the fact that suffering arises from the disobedience to the laws and commandments of God and from this disobedience all the world's ills derive. When Franco says he hears someone ordering him to stay in bed because the salvation of his family and his country depends on this, he is not delusional, he is letting this primordial drama become present. With the same rationality with which his Catholic psychiatrist prescribes drugs to him, he could also try to help him carry this cross and share such responsibility. But

> *"A psychiatrist has been trained to believe that, if he was to think that he thinks and feels more or less like those people that he diagnosed with psychosis, that does not mean that they are not psychotic, but that he is psychotic himself. There is, in a sense, a greater difference between a psychiatrist who believes this and a schizophrenic than between a normal human being and a mouse.*
>
> *Differences between people, not 'different' people"* (R.D.LAING 1982, p. 36)

But what did Adam and Eve do? Why was it so important that they did not eat the apple? The knowledge of good and evil, the conquest of free will and self-consciousness, coincide with the loss of the situation of communion with the rest of creation. No coincidence that immediately after eating the apple and sinning Adam and Eve discover their body, their individuality, their limits and their border, realizing that they are naked and being ashamed of this. The expulsion from Eden is equivalent to the biological birth: unity is broken and we incarnate into a body of which we remain prisoners. The *voices* are in some way echoes of that world we have lost forever, they are rooted in that primal experience during which we did not exist yet. In the beginning, in fact, was the *Word*.

The thesis that the experience of *hearing voices* can somehow be considered the vestiges of an era in which human consciousness, as we know it, was not born yet, was developed and proposed by an experimental psychologist, Julian JAYNES, who exposed it in his book The Origin of Consciousness in the Breakdown of the Bicameral Mind (J. JAYNES, 1984). In it, he essentially argues that the consciousness that we believe is inherent to human beings is rather a fairly recent product of human evolution. He states that *"... there was a time when human nature was split into two parts: a directive one called god, and a subject part called man"* (J.JAYNES 1984, p. 111). A time when *hearing voices* was the norm. Human beings were guided by a system of *voices* that intervened on every occasion when it was necessary to make a decision. According to this author who developed his ideas through the analysis of documents and archaeological finds relating to civilizations such as the Greek, the Egyptian, the Aztec... the experience of *hearing voices* is nothing but the activation of an archaic and universal mode of brain functioning. No pathological alteration, then, but the recovery of human capacities and possibilities which fell into disuse with the birth of consciousness.

Consciousness has replaced, according to Jaynes, the directive *voice* of the gods which would evaluate, command, foresee the events and choose what to do. The *inner dialogue* that constitutes the essence of our being conscious is an evolution of the *dialogue* we had with the gods. We have in other words *internalized* this relationship, identifying with the *voice* that spoke to us and making it our own.

JAYNES, in any case, has no doubts with regards to the *reality* of the voices.

"Some people find it difficult to even imagine that there can be mental voices that are heard with the same experiential quality as externally produced voices. After all, there is neither a mouth nor a larynx in the brain!

Whatever brain areas are utilized, it is absolutely certain that such voices do exist and that experiencing them is just like hearing actual sound" (J.JAYNES 1984, p. 113).

The need to develop a system of articulated *voices* comes from the urgency to achieve an adaptation to the natural and human environment in which humans were included. The first spoken orders by those who were appointed as chiefs or kings, in order to become the norm and rule of life, had somehow to be *heard* again and again by those who had to adapt to them. There was nothing at the dawn of human history that would allow men, according to JAYNES, to use skills which, we believe today, constitute our consciousness (memory, learning by trial and error, forecasting abilities ...). These functions were performed by *voices* that every member of the community would hear and that regulated social life.

Besides the cultural *evidence*, JAYNES gives us an *organic* hypothesis of the origin of the voices. He believes that the phenomenon of *hearing voices* may be a function of the today unused areas of the brain. In particular, he identifies an area of the right hemisphere of our brain, corresponding to the language area of the left hemisphere. Here once the *voices* of the gods were harbored, who would speak to the left hemisphere, commanding men what to do.

This area, if electrically stimulated, produces auditory experiences in humans that are very close to those described by people who hear *voices*. This is of course not enough to prove anything for sure. Nevertheless, it raises the prospect of an integrated study of *voices* that interprets them from the point of view of their *positive* function of process of perception and understanding of reality, as well as from the point of view of the biochemical processes that make this modality possible.

JAYNES shows, in my opinion, that one can do serious research on the experience of *voices*, even from the biological point of view, without necessarily using the misleading concept of *illness*. *Hearing voices* can be considered a process of functioning of our brain and our consciousness: identifying it, that is, with a particular mode of human knowledge and existence. Not a disorder in the functioning of a *normal* brain and perception, but a *different* perception that is *possible* and genetically and culturally inborn in our brains.

The fact that it is a human experience which is in line with the way our body *can* work, does not mean that it can be lived with the strength of a true cataclysm by those who experience it. Bound as we are to a culture and a reference model that sees our consciousness as distinct from other people's consciousness and our body as the ultimate limit between us and the world, we can't help feeling *crazy* in front of an experience that we believe is *impossible*. Understanding that for a long time *hearing voices* was the normal way human beings lived and took their decisions, may help us to face the terror and the fear that such an experience, often in the early stages, causes us to feel.

Definitely not enough, but it is a good way to start.

The fear of going crazy and / or being considered mad, is the feeling that drives us more than any other into the, often deadly, embrace of psychiatry. The fear, together with the attempt to *rationalise* it. As one *voice hearer* states:

"It seemed as if I had phone lines inside my chest. Initially, I was even foolish enough to look inside my shirt to see where they came from - maybe there was a microphone or something like that, I thought, 'amazing, it seems to me I have a built-in telephone switchboard'" (M.A.J. ROMME, A.D.M.A.C ESCHER 1988)

Rationalizations of this kind, such attempts to explain the *voices* in a meaningful way and from our *scientific* knowledge of reality, have the paradoxical effect of making us appear totally irrational and foolish in the eyes of most. So happens to the lady that presses charges against her neighbours because they speak to her from electrical appliances; or to the other lady holding up the TV volume so as not to hear them. All the *rational* explanations or strategies we use to deny or silence the voices, in one way or another turn against us. Probably the level of reality in which they exist and operate is not controlled by our senses and by the instruments at our disposal. So it should be explained to the lady that one can't arrest the *voices* and take them to Court, as well as there is no sound that can drown them out as hearing them seems to be something more radical than just perceiving them with our ears.

JAYNES mentions in this regard the research carried out on deaf people diagnosed with schizophrenia. *"In one study, 16 of 22 profoundly deaf schizophrenics who suffered from hallucinations, claimed to have heard some form of communication. A woman of thirty-two, born deaf, who was tormented by remorse for having undergone a therapeutic abortion, said to have* heard *accusations from God. Another woman, fifty years old, suffering from congenital deafness, heard supernatural voices proclaiming that she had occult powers."* (JAYNES pp.119-120.) This shows according to the author that the perception of voices is cerebral rather than sensory. Which from the point of view of the existential experience, is equivalent to say that *hearing voices* is very similar to the feeling of being inhabited, possessed or controlled by others.

We are dealing with words that, yes, have all the sonic characteristics of human language, but that somehow seem quiet and intimate as our thoughts are. In fact they are not heard by others as well as the thoughts are not and, for the most part, respond *telepathically* not only to what we yell at them, but also and especially to what we think, the emotions we feel, the ideas we develop. The resulting experience is very similar to what we think a telepathic experience should be. The feeling is as if we *hear* the thoughts of others and we communicate with them through our minds.

The *voices* literally break into our head. Their nature is such as to allow them to sneak into the most intimate recesses of our inner life. They can mingle with our thoughts, follow us in our dreams, know our most intimate secrets. Their power in fact comes from the knowledge that they seem to have of any of our smallest wound. Our weakness rises, conversely, from the fact that often we do not know anything about them and their objective. Increasing our awareness and our understanding of what it means to *hear voices*, helps us to have more and more power and energy to control them.

This is at least what common sense would suggest when you are faced with a situation or experience that you do not understand. Common sense, indeed. Psychiatry is not a product of common sense, but of fear. Its interest is not understanding, but controlling. The man who walks around the theater looking for the thread, from which the music that everyone else pretends not to hear is coming, is disturbing the show and unnerving the audience. Although the music he hears can't be stopped, he can be grabbed and taken to the emergency room of the nearest hospital for help.

What *help* do you think that man needs? If we really believed in what he says, we could respond in the same way we respond to a guy who asks for information about the nearest bar. We can be annoyed, but nevertheless we do not think that he is *crazy*. The help that they both need is information about something they seek. The difference is not *in* them, but in our judgment on whether what they are looking for exists or not.

It is this difference that transforms the human experience in pathology. Being sad because of a loss, for example, is considered a *normal* occurrence. But if we remain in this condition for a period that is longer than the norm defined by psychiatry, our sadness turns into an *illness*. Psychiatry demarcates the limits of time and space within which we can move and express our feelings. If for any reason we do not respect them, it builds material, chemical, or symbolic *prisons*, where it locks us in and prevents our *insanity* from infecting others.

In the case of *voices* in particular, the psychiatric reasoning causes people to reject what they are hearing and consider it a pure product of an altered biochemistry or psychology. The therapeutic prescriptions will go from keeping patients busy with all sorts of activities, to the intake of substances that limit their ability to think, feel and act; from hospitalization in a psychiatric ward to psychotherapy designed to show them the groundlessness and the non-existence of their perceptions.

The entire psychiatric system is constructed so as to act, with or without people's consent, by dismissing their experiences and by limiting their possibility of communication. After all, so long as psychiatry identifies the *symptoms* of the illness it claims it is treating, with people's choices, ideas and ways of acting, it can only appear, in the eyes of those who suffer, in the same way as a real social persecution.

Treating identifies in fact, in psychiatric practice, with *punishing*: people are punished for what they say they are seeing and hearing, hoping that they cease to do so or, in any case, they cease to communicate it. They are punished both with admissions within psychiatric wards and facilities, and also, above all, turning their existence into a life of probation; both with the use of substances or therapies that limit their judgment and their will, and also, most importantly, trapping them into the role of the foolish, unreliable and in/credible *ill*.

That's it, I believe that the core of the psychiatric power arises from the destruction of the credibility of his patients. The less they are credible, the more the psychiatrists are authorized to intervene and impose their point of view and treatment. Often the moment when we come into contact with psychiatry, we still maintain a minimum of credibility that gives us a minimum of power in the management of our choices. After that contact we lose, officially, every possibility to act, and at the same time, others acquire total control of our lives.

JAYNES suggests that this attitude of confrontation that psychiatry has towards the experience of *hearing voices*, with massive and invasive interventions in the mind and in the existence of individuals, hides in fact a struggle for the control of individuals. The *voices* and psychiatry share the same objective and justify themselves in the same way: everything they do is *for* our own sake. JAYNES in fact writes: "*At the first suspicion of hallucinations, psychotics are administered some kind of drug, such as Thorazine, which specifically eliminates hallucinations. Such an approach is questionable to say the least and it may not be beneficial for the patient, but it may for the hospital, who wishes to eliminate this antagonistic control on the patient.*"(JAYNES J. 1984, p. 115)

In this clash it is not difficult that the *voices* often prevail, at the very least because the *dialogue* with them, no matter how hard and distressing, is much more sensible and meaningful than the *monologue* which psychiatry seeks to impose on us. Often the *voices* are the only form of communication and inter-human relationship that psychiatric practice allows us. In asylums, for example, the *voices* are often the only human realities that are present. Nurses, doctors, social workers are an integral part of the railings and peeling walls: deaf and dumb witnesses to be soiled with feces, spit and anger.

The power that the *voices* have over our choices also comes from this isolation that psychiatry exposes us to. Physical but also, especially, emotional and relational isolation. No one is available anymore to listen to us, to talk about what happens to us. Among the instructions that are given to our family and friends there is to *control* and make sure that we don't restart to hear voices or to act as if we heard them.

The fact that we don't talk about what the *voices* say, even though it is hailed by psychiatrists and those who are close to us as a proof of the improvement of our mental condition, prevents any dialogue between the voices' *truth* and the *reality* in which we live. We all know that it is thanks to this dialogue and this relational mediation that we manage to form our opinions and we avoid, as much as possible, being rigid in our fixed, beyond criticism, ideas. We must say that holding onto *certainty* is never pathological, but it's a human necessity. Coming to the conclusion of believing I was really chosen by god for an *impossible* mission is not very different to being convinced of the existence of a universal incestuous desire that involves our relationship with our parents. And yet in the first case we don't hesitate to talk about *delusion*, whereas we call scientific *certainty* the Oedipus complex developed by Freud.

The problem in my view is not that, by listening to the voices *only*, you end up convinced of the legitimacy of killing John Lennon or the possibility of being able to fly, thus risking your life. We run the same risks by listening to our parents, teachers, poets, generals and all other material people who are around us. The issue is to allow everyone to have that dialogue, which can in itself avoid that our need to have *certainty* will result in the destruction of the certainties of others.

Any theory that denies *dialogue* with the voices is, in my opinion, impliedly complicit for the foolish and contradictory actions that derive from it. The man who looks for the thread, from which the music he hears is coming, would have no need to destroy the theater with a sledgehammer, if we were to allow and, rather, help him to unravel this mystery.

We are willing to accept that the lack of *dialogue* is what most hurts human beings, only to impose it regardless to some and call it *therapy*. Even that surrogate of human relationships that we call *psychotherapy* basically denies what it states in theory. Even in that case there isn't a real and genuine *dialogue*. All that listening hides the secret attempt to convince us that something is wrong in our perceptions and make us accept *treatment*. In this, as in all other fields in which it operates, psychiatry aims to push people to *betray* themselves, to deny their own ideas and experiences, to submit to its point of view. In the case of *voices* this results in an attempt to replace a *dialogue* full of emotions and feelings, with a senseless and useless *monologue*.

The psychiatric hypothesis goes far beyond any other human theory in denying the existence and reality of *voices*. Not only it does not believe that there is someone who is speaking to us, but it does not even believe that we're *really* hearing them.

What fades as a result of this attitude is not so much or just the possibility of some form of human relationship with those who hear *voices*, but rather the possibility of their existence as persons. In the face of psychiatric practices the warning that R.D. Laing launches from the pages of his book, *The Politics of Experience*, is still current:

> *"Before we can ask such an optimistic question as <What is a personal relationship?>, we have to ask if a personal relationship is possible, or,* **are persons possible** *in our present situation?"* (R.D.LAING 1980, p. 19)

This attitude, aside from the arbitrary judgment it expresses, is, in fact, as far removed as it can be from the desire to give help to someone. The paradoxical mechanism that is triggered by the psychiatric judgment is what makes us believe that, as *voices* are an imaginary fact, even the fear, terror or anxiety that result from them are themselves a fantasy.

By denying people's experience we expose them to an ever greater terror, without limits and with no possible exit. If the door is not barred by the *voices* that threaten us out there, it's the nurses who prevent us from moving and defending ourselves. Think about what it means, for those who are persecuted by a voice that threatens to kill them, being locked in a room, among unknown people, unable to escape, to move, to even just listen to music, to shout, to stomp their feet on the ground, to leave the water running, to recite a chant or to do anything else that can help ward off the threat. This is what commonly happens to those who are hospitalized in a psychiatric facility.

These men and women are not believed. There being no threat, all their actions are foolish and should be banned. The *cure* is to prevent people from doing exactly what could help them. Psychiatry does not take into account the information coming from its *in*voluntary victims. On the contrary, it considers that an integral part of the disease that it intends to cure. If Anna is sitting in a corner repeating his chant and keeping the man's hands that dishonour her at bay, psychiatry takes her away as the police do with Cesare every time he lies down on the ground at the train station. It rips them out of what it believes are meaningless actions and delusional crises, to drown them with a drip or make them sit around a table to draw butterflies.

What remains of a human being, if all his emotions, his choices, his desires, his actions and his thoughts are regarded as fantasies or delusions? What remains of a person if his story and his life is narrated and managed by others?

To think that a theory and a practice, which systematically destroys the subjectivity of people and denies meaning to their experiences, can help anyone is pure madness. It's a fabrication in which we must believe in order to avoid facing the fear and terror that we impose to these men and women who are guilty only of being and communicating what they are. No *illness* inhabits them. They live, like every other human being, in accordance with their own opinions and to reach some goals. The fact that we do not agree with them or they seem *impossible* to us, can't justify that we consider them the result of delusional fantasies. We owe them the same respect that we would have liked for Giordano Bruno or Galileo, for all those who expressed (or will express) a different view of reality, in disagreement with the shared one.

The only possible way to the future arises from *divergences* and *differences* like these. We can't let our fear slow down and frustrate our search for *truth*. Especially because, in this undeclared war, we leave the best of us on the battlefield. Those who dare (or are thrown) to explore beyond the known universe.

There is an idea that runs through all the movements of criticism of psychiatry, both the institutional and the instinctive psychiatry, arisen by the survival instinct: if people were left to themselves, that is, if they were listened to and helped according to their directions and if knowledge were derived directly from their experiences, they almost certainly would find the door that allows free access to and returning from the *other* world which they found themselves catapulted in. It's what some psychiatrists call it *spontaneous healing* and that, according to BATESON, could constitute a rule if people did not collide *"...in family life or in hospitals, with grossly unfavorable circumstances so that they can't defend themselves even with the richest and best organized hallucinatory experience..."* (BATESON G., op. cit. R.D. Laing, 1980, p. 118).

R.D.LAING goes even further. Considering that psychiatry itself is part of the problem rather than a solution, he proposes that *"Instead of the degrading ceremony of a psychiatric consultation, diagnosis and prognosis, there is the need for those who are ready for it (and that, in psychiatric terminology, are often those who are about to develop schizophrenia), of a ceremony of initiation, during which the individual is guided, with each and every legality and encouragement of society, through inner space and time, by people who have already been there and made it back. Psychiatrically, this would appear as ex-patients helping future patients to go mad".* (RD Laing 1980, p. 128)

These ideas, far from being expression of the revolutionary attitude of some eccentric psychiatrist, belong to all those who have been and are the subject of psychiatrists' attention. There is no patient who hasn't at least once thought they were not in front of a doctor or a treatment, but a sheer violence. There is no patient who has not experienced the debasement of all their opinions. There is no patient who has not thought they could do on their own.

Today, while psychiatry reunites around the old slogans (mental illnesses are illnesses of the brain), the tendency to self-organization of psychiatric patients grows ever stronger as they are beginning to get their voices heard, especially with regards to how their behaviours are defined and the way in which their experiences need to be dealt with.

It is not uncommon to come across, in the United States as well as in Europe, groups that call themselves *survivors* who defend their rights claiming the *fact* that they are not *sick* and the right to organize themselves to deal with the emergence of their own experiences. The main purpose of these groups is the one expressed above by LAING, people want to help and be helped to become mad without this meaning the end of them as human beings or of the possibility to live on this side or that side of the imaginary line that we have drawn between reality and fantasy.

The *lack of insight into the illness* - which is still the flag behind which the most heinous crimes against humanity lurk, perpetrated in psychiatric facilities around the world -becomes again for the *survivors* what has always been: their claim of being persons, individuals, human beings. Today we know that the millions of our fellow human beings who have suffered (and suffer) the psychiatric barbarism of the mental asylums, described as *irresponsible* because they resisted the lobotomy as well as the electroshock, insulin coma and psychotropic drugs, have struggled against their physical and psychological destruction. We should always keep this in mind when we hear today that psychiatric patients do not realize that they need care. We should have the humility and humanity to learn something from our history.

After all one just needs a little common sense to draw the conclusions to which M.A.J. ROMME has come - a Dutch social psychiatrist who for some years has been bringing forward, inside of the psychiatric establishment, a *new* approach to the issue of *voices*. It is new and revolutionary only for psychiatrists themselves who have always refused to learn from experience, insisting with their inhuman attempt to prove their theses.

The idea was born almost by accident. ROMME noticed that one of his patients, who had been hearing *voices* from the age of 14, had been hospitalized several times and subjected to various pharmacological and psychological therapies, seemed to find some benefit in the management of her *voices* from a theory she had developed since she read JAYNES's book. As a good psychiatrist he decided to use what, to him, must have seemed to be a strategy to try and break the isolation in which the experience of the *voices* had forced his patient, making her more and more *sensibly* contemplate the possibility of suicide: he would have encouraged her relationship and dialogue with other people who were *hearing voices*. ROMME and his patient appeared in a popular Dutch television program asking people who heard *voices* to make contact with them.

What happened next changed their plans and opened unexpected perspectives. As in any case in which we are willing to listen to what others have to say about their experiences, ROMME found that not all the people who *hear voices* are regarded or treated as mad and - this had always been denied by psychiatry - it was possible to live together, evolve and grow in spite of the *voices*, thanks to the *voices* and through the *voices*. Along with the people who could not in any way understand and communicate with their voices, also thanks to the work of psychiatric miseducation, a large group (150 out of 450 contacts) declared themselves capable of managing and using the relationship with their *voices* in an evolutionary way.

The questionnaires that ROMME sent to those who had responded to the invitation showed a different reality from the one that the books of psychiatry pass off as scientific truth. Not only that, it also became clear that there was something perverse in the way he himself as a psychiatrist, until then, had considered the issue and dealt with it.

20 of those *voice hearers*, who appeared more confident about their *dialogue* with the voices, were invited by ROMME to lecture to an audience of 300 *voice hearers*. Directly facing these experiences, he identified a number of features that seemed present in almost all experiences.

The first and, in my opinion, the most important feature, is the individual and collective *context* in which *dialogue* takes place with the voices. What appears to us as an eminently inner experience is decisively influenced by the human and cultural environment in which it takes place. If we place the experience that we live in a shared cultural context, the *dialogue* that follows will not make us afraid, as the spiritualists are not scared when they hear the *voice* of a deceased person. That which happens to us acquires the dimension of a known/familiar experience and becomes an integral part of our identity. Not only that. Our experience can be socialized, a bit like what happens to those who hear the messages of the Virgin Mary and become spiritual representatives and a destination for pilgrimage, acquiring the importance of a modality of knowledge and experience to be considered.

In the next chapter I will outline some of these experiences of *dialogue* with the voices. What should be clear is that our response to the message of the *voices*, as well as the reaction of the social context in which we live, is critical in determining the evolution of the experience itself. It can lead to *holiness* if shared or to *madness* if rejected: it can be described as a *gift* if understood or endured as an *illness* if denied. The inability to manage the *voices* is not inherent to the very nature of this experience. As for the management of any inter-human relationship, it is related to individual characteristics, our history and culture, and expectations of the social environment and family who live around us.

The stories of the *voice hearers*, as they appeared to ROMME, described the three possible phases that seemed relevant to the management of *voices*, as follows:

1. *a sudden episode experienced as frightening, in other words, the startling phase;*

2. *a process of selection and communication with the voices, i.e. the phase of organization;*

3. *a period in which one achieves a more stable approach, the so-called stabilization phase.* (M.A.J. ROMME and A.D.M.A.C. ESHER 1988)

It is obvious that a lot is at stake in the first phase in which the surprise and fear of what is happening to us may lead us to a series of choices and behaviour that are difficult to control. Yet, in the face of the emergence of these *voices*, we do not have an infinite range of alternatives. We can talk about them, running the risk of being treated as visionary and crazy (in precisely the same way we would ourselves treat anyone who revealed to us such an experience); we can withhold the truth and remain prisoners of the fear of being discovered; we can communicate with them trying to figure out what they want from us.

None of these options is completely feasible. The idea of keeping the secret, for example, is not easy and is likely to escalate in us a number of uncontrollable and invincible fears. As a *voice hearer* states:

The hard part was that people would never have admitted to being in telepathic contact with me. At first I did not dare to say it, but after a while I did. The voices had a strong influence on my private life and this made me angry, so I thought: what the heck, I'll come and tell you, you are in telepathic contact with me, I want you to admit it. But they would always reply: no, it is not so, really. And then I thought that they had formed a sort of conspiracy against me. (M.A.J. ROMME and A.D.M.A.C ESHER 1988)

Moreover, in a case like this, we are stuck in a paradox. Revealing to others that we hear their *voice* or that we can perceive, somehow, their thoughts, exposes us directly to their and psychiatry's judgment. Conversely silence can make us gradually so suspicious that we are prevented from any possibility of interpersonal relationship. As we can't expect that others will confirm what we are hearing, we can hardly avoid thinking, given the clarity and sharpness of our experience, that they do have something to hide.

I believe that there is no greater difficulty than that of being able to manage an experience that connects us with the *voices* of people who are close to us. It sends us into such a mess that we can hardly avoid the inconsistencies in behaviour that betray us in the eyes of others. In those cases, it becomes difficult if not impossible to distinguish the things that are *said* by those we *hear*, resulting in relational impasse.

Whom should we believe? Which of the *two* voices is telling the truth? The *voice* that sends me his thoughts telepathically or the one that denies this transmission? The issue is further complicated by the nature of the relationship we have with the other, even *before* hearing their voice. The things we hear *telepathically* will be more credible as we believe they are *true*, that is, corresponding to the idea that we have of ourselves or we think others have of us.

It is not the voice that convinces us: it only confirms a truth that is already *within* us. The issue that arises can't be dismissed as an *imaginary* thing because it's suggested by an *imaginary* voice. The issue is real and must be addressed in the reality of our relationship with the other.

After all, who feels like excluding the possibility that there may be a *telepathic* communication between us and others, of which we have no awareness? And what prevents us from attempting to recognize *voices* that others hear as our thoughts? Instead of denying this possibility, it should be investigated in depth the *truth* that is inherent in the things that others hear from us even though we are sure that we have not opened our mouth. This joint research with those who hear *voices* allows us to recover a series of thoughts, feelings and emotions and allows them to learn how to select them and discern between the various messages that they perceive about us.

Occasionally it's happened to me I've being accused for things that I *told* people I had not seen for days. The instinctive reaction was to deny everything, as the things that they had heard seemed so far away from me and my way of thinking. So you don't believe me?! This was the answer of the person who would accuse me.

It's easy to believe the *voices* someone hears when they are the voices of others. If someone comes and tells you that yesterday he heard your voice inviting him to go kill his psychiatrist, certainly your instinct is to deny the authorship of that thought, explicitly stating that he invented everything or that he imagined he heard your *voice* in order to justify his desire and his inner will.

Experiences of this kind happen to all of those who presume they are able to accept that the voices are *real*. It's as if the *voices* test us in front of the person we say we are able to, and want to understand.

Our reaction is as good as that of psychiatrists specialised in psychotherapy, who in theory claim to be willing to understand the *truth* of the experiences of others, and that, in practice, do not accept that those others can question them in any way. The psychiatric descriptions are not dissimilar to those of the psychiatrist who makes a diagnosis of schizophrenia based on the presence, in the behavior of the patient, of *unmotivated laughter*. That makes him assume that the person *hears voices* and is, therefore, hallucinated. Not for a moment the psychiatrist can accept that one is actually laughing at him. The psychiatrist in question trembled as he asked the girl if she felt nervous. The girl laughed, because she found it funny that this trembling and anxious man would ask her if she felt nervous, but her laughter was, apparently, *unmotivated*.

On the other hand, this psychiatrist was no less human or attentive than his colleagues; he, like them, in that moment of diagnostic orgasm was no longer a man, he was the *norm*, the one and only possible truth.

If you do not speak with a psychiatrist, it does not mean that you believe he is a mediocre or overpowering man, but that you have an autistic attitude; if you throw a punch at the nurse who bars the ward door and stops you from going out, you're not trying to regain your freedom, you are acting out; if you say you are not sick you do not express the fact that you feel good as you are, you lack of insight; and so on.

The fate and future of the girl is not determined by the outcome of a hypothetical illness, it rather depends on the attitude that she will hold in respect of her *therapy* and her *therapists*. The problem has nothing to do with malice or sadism of some psychiatrists; it is instead akin to every psychiatric practice. The fact that they have self-proclaimed therapists and scholars of human vicissitudes, places psychiatrists in a role where all our resistance to their work can only be experienced as something foolish and ill. How can one refuse a *therapy* they swear it heals all the anxieties, fears and make the *voices* fall silent?

The fact that the vast majority of psychiatric patients refuse psychiatric diagnoses and therapies has historically been seen as *proof* of their illness, except they are proven to be right with the distance of some decades. What if there was instead something wrong in the psychiatric (con)science?

I must confess that, looking *inside* me and *in* the relationship I had with the *voice hearer* of the day, I have always come to recognise those words, if not as mine, as my *possibilities* or possibilities of our relationship. Every time my *voice*, heard by the other without my knowledge, has added something to the understanding of our relationship, my thoughts and his desires. It's become part of us and our story: not my *voice*, not his *voice*, but an event that reveals us both.

By the way no one has ever killed his psychiatrist. Also because we have learned together how to go without doing it.

Communicating *with* the voices and communicating *the* voices is, basically, the only possible strategy to prevent them driving us mad, or worse, driving us to psychiatry. The experience of ROMME's 150 listeners confirmed that one does not need (or it is even harmful) to pretend not to hear the voices; that attempting to keep busy or distracted is a huge and unnecessary effort; that the use of legal and illegal substances does not silence the voices but it compresses and desertifies our inner world.

"The most successful strategy described by people who were hearing voices, was to select the positive voices and hear and talk to just them, trying to understand them." (M.A.J. ROMME, A.D.M.A.C. ESCHER 1988)

It seems the obvious solution, but it is a Copernican revolution for those who, like psychiatrists, tend to psychiatrize and pathologize every human experience. *Hearing voices* is like falling in love. We do not always find the right person; sometimes we come across some wrong relationship that makes us suffer and leads us to act in ways that are not ordinary. Nevertheless, we are not yet able to define 'falling in love' as a *mental illness*. Although nothing stops it from ending up becoming one.

Mental illnesses are not discovered, nor even can they be eradicated; they simply begin or cease to be regarded as such. Nothing prevents that, in the near future, falling in love will be regarded as a plague, and that, on the contrary, *hearing voices* will return to have, for example, the social purpose of controlling the mind and body of men that, according to Jaynes, it had at the origin of human civilization.

After all it's been years that not only psychiatric research, but also politics, war and advertising, attempt to define the mechanisms that regulate the complex system of human consciousness, in order to discover ways to affect more and more radically its operation. To convince people to behave in a certain way is a very difficult and risky undertaking. Nevertheless, it is necessary for psychiatry, as well as for advertising, for the State... that this happens.

In this phase of *democratization*, psychiatry does not look to impose its presence, but rather to develop in individuals the *consciousness* of the necessity of its existence. After all for psychiatry it has always been decisive to try and convince their patients, not only to act as *ill*, but to feel so.

The selection of positive *voices*, and the *dialogue* with them, is a heritage of the mystical experience of every age and culture. The Christians call it *discernment*, and it is, in my opinion, the only sensible way to deal with this experience. One accepts the *reality* of what one is hearing, and one chooses between what comes from God or what comes from the devil, what leads to good or to evil urges, what helps us or destroys us ... One makes a choice, like for every human communication, in favor of what one finds credible, acceptable, right...

Discernment is an ethical and not scientific fact. The mystics do not deny the reality of their experience, and so do the *lay* voice hearers that are able to manage them. They simply choose among the various opinions and presences those whom they consider reliable, useful, comprehensive... depending on their needs, their story, their character.

In order to do this it is important that the person overcomes any prejudice about his sanity and the reality of his perceptions. Not only should those around his/her learn to have respect for this experience and help manage discerning what is good from what is bad. One must *educate* his/her perception: learning to open and close the communication, defending one's subjectivity and one's own inner space, discerning between oneself and the voices.

"Those who have been able to manage their voices have developed some kind of balance. During this stabilization process, the individual gets to see the voices as part of oneself. Voices are perceived as part of life and have a positive influence. In this stage the individual is able to choose whether to follow the directions of the voices or their own ideas." (M.A.J. ROMME, A.D.M.A.C. ESHER 1988)

Regarding the psychiatric approach, ROMME clearly states that, at present, all assumptions about the *pathological* nature of this experience are not productive from the point of view of either the explanation or the management of the problems that arise with *hearing voices* that others do not hear.

According to ROMME the mental health professionals who come into contact with those who *hear voices* should:

> a. *Accept that the patient really hears the voices. Voices which are more powerful than sensory perceptions.*
>
> b. *Try to understand the language they use to describe their framework and the language that the voices use to communicate. (...)*
>
> c. *Help the patient to structure time and space in the management of voices, then build the communication with the voices, in other words encourage the distinction between the positive and the negative voices. (...)*
>
> d. *Encourage the patient to meet other people and encourage him / her to read on the subject of hearing voices; this can reduce both the taboo and the isolation. (M.A.J. ROMME, A.D.M.A.C ESHER 1988)*

That is, they should stop being who they are and doing what they are commissioned to do.

The fact remains that the 150 voice hearers of ROMME, just like the mystics, found their way on their own, with passion and tenacity. They ran the risk of being excluded forever from their social and emotional life, and I do not think that there is any concrete reason to risk their existence again by relying on psychiatric *care*.

Moreover, our ability to manage our vital functions and our social life is acquired slowly by trial and error, and often at the price of grievous suffering. There is no reason to get rid of the voices just because we suffer not knowing how to manage them. Just like a *voice hearer* clarifies:

"If you fall off your bike you do not throw it away, but you keep putting yourself in right relation with it. You dream up a

beautiful bike ride as best as you can, in yourself. At the end of the day I feel I am neither the winner nor the loser, but it's as if another dimension has been added to my life. A dimension that you can manage and that eventually may be helpful." (M.AJ. ROMME, A.D.M.A.C ESHER 1988)

In the next chapter we will discuss some of these passengers of the unknown.

DIALOGUE

Tonight very sleepy, very sleepy yesterday too,
but tonight it seemed to me that I was hearing voices
that I couldn't distinguish, and I turned the radio on to
not hear them.
This morning in the kitchen, while making coffee, I
heard:
<< with your radio we could not sleep >>
(Sara)

The *voices*, then, seem to have an independent mind, their own will, their own consciousness and memory. Experiences like those of Sara show that it's not possible to dismiss the *voices* as mere products of our altered biochemistry or as projection of our unconscious desires.

The *voices* think, feel, remember, and act, like each of us, to achieve a goal or to avoid a hazard. The *voices* do not sleep if you keep the radio turned on. Paradoxically, this technique used by many voice hearers looking for a sound that manages to drown them out, just keeps them often awake and pissed off. So even when you are able to fall asleep, when you wake up you will find them there again, even more cruel and vindictive than before.

The refusal to *dialogue* with the voices, it has been already said, is not a step forward on the path of rational knowledge of the world; it is rather a cultural strategy to cope with the terror and the crisis that this and other such experiences open in our social and mental order.

Dialoguing with the voices, in fact, may *mean* ceasing to be who others expect us to be, ceasing to act in compliance with shared moral, social and criminal norms and laws, ceasing to confirm, with our existence and identity, the existence and identity of others: in other words, escaping the *control* of our minds and our actions. This does not mean necessarily being *free*, but rather no longer being subject to the limitations of the shared reality.

That's probably what makes the people we call *madmen* more *dangerous* in our eyes than those we call *criminals*. Somehow we feel that the criminals, in breaking the law, confirm their existence and the existence of a shared reality. The madmen instead appear to act devoid of any known purpose, upsetting the order of what we consider real. If we know what to expect from a *criminal*, we remain puzzled at the universe of possibilities and radicality that are brought in front of us by a *madman*.

Francis of Assisi on the roofs is not very far from Giorgio who was forced to get off the bus with which he had decided to crash into a wall (in accordance with the shared version) or better, with which he had decided to get through a wall (according to his own version). They are no different if only because at the basis of their actions there is the perception that reality, the way we describe it, does not exist. Not only that. They are very similar with regards to the crisis that they open in our system of social control. They have broken the law but without *malice*. They should be controlled but one can't give them the status of sensible people. They are not criminals because they *can't* be: if we considered them as such we would have to take their *motives* and their *reasons* seriously, we would have to recognize their existence.

It must not be overlooked that Francis, as well as George, commits another *crime* that goes unpunished: in rejecting his identity and his role in society, he upsets the identity of those nearby. It should be investigated in depth how it feels to be mothers, fathers and siblings of a saint or of someone that professes to be one. Surely we would not just find the social distress that this exposes us to, but a profound disorientation due to our relative's explicit rejection of being what we expect him/her to be. If George ceases to be a good family man, not only he endangers the economic situation of his children, he also, above all, shatters the mental order of all those who have built their identity and sense of their actions on his role and function as a father and a husband.

Lina, when she manages to escape psychiatric persecution, goes around stations and universities claiming to be 25 years old and that her name is Olga, talking about her parents in Milan, and she claims to be a medical student. In *reality* (in the *shared* reality) it seems she is older than forty and her parents are both retired elderly Sicilians. She breaks the law, Lina. She travels around without a ticket. Not only that. She refuses to recognize her family as *her own*. Her son is her brother. She is never married, she has never suffered the indignity and violence of the man they claim he is the father of those 2 sons of hers. They are perhaps the children and the life of Lina, not *hers*. Olga has a different life, has other perspectives.

I can clearly hear the thoughts that come into our mind when we hear stories like this. We believe that the pain and the violence of her husband have brought Lina to *repress* the years and the identity she lived with him. In order not to suffer she has like *invented* a story and a parallel life, which she has come to believe. I'm not saying that this reasoning does not make *sense* or cannot be agreed with. I just believe that such an idea, though born from the desire to understand Lina, paradoxically leads to *inhuman* consequences.

By defining *illusory* the new identity of Lina, we explicitly deny its existence and tend to bring Olga in the body and in the life of who she is not anymore, and probably never was. What we call the acceptance of reality is nothing but imposing, at times blindly, the idea we have of the life and the reality of others. Olga can't be anybody other than Lina. Even though we know that the life of Lina is not worth living, she will have to return to live it, because this is *reality*. Our only concern is that she agrees to be the one we believe she is.

Our identity does not necessarily coincide with the facts or the visible choices of our social existence. If there is a certificate or witnesses to prove the fact that Lina is married, it is not possible that she claims she isn't. In *fact* it is possible to be not married even though one has sent the invitations, has got into a church, has bought a house and has gone on a honeymoon trip. Being married also implies *feeling* married. We can live this and other life events without taking part in them. A bit like what the prisoners of concentration camps or involuntary patients of psychiatric wards around the world do.

If we go back to Francis of Assisi it will then be clear that the transformations that can occur in us are of such a nature that they are able to radically supplant every identity of ours. Francis was no longer the young son of the mercer of Assisi, he was no longer the warrior, the heir to the family assets. Just like Lina, now, somehow, he knew he had never been that. His true nature and identity was revealed only now with his nakedness on the street. Francesco getting undressed is not only the representation of poverty, chosen as a way of life, but it is primarily a renunciation of the social identity he was wearing and in which he found himself hiding (or trapped).

The transformation of Francis, as we know, was first tolerated and then accepted by everybody, even if it broke, symbolically and materially, the family and social order in which he was included. We can sensibly assume that if we allowed Lina to be free to be Olga, she would be able, like Francis, to build a life that is certainly more sensible than the coerced one which is forced upon her by psychiatric and family *care*. Yet today this seems *impossible* to accept.

There are radical transformations of our personal identity which in any way can find a balance with the social expectations around us, even before birth. Nevertheless, we can't deprive them of their value and of the respect we owe to every human being, regardless of *who* he considers himself to be. We owe the same respect and the same attention to Lina and to Olga. While sharing the same body, they are two different people, with different sensitivity, history, desires. Or, rather, Lina is the person that our gaze and our expectations have built, Olga is what she *is*.

Dissociation is not *inside* Lina, but *between* her and us. With the same arbitrariness with which we say that she lost herself, we could say that we are the ones who have never known her. The fact that today she may *need* to be Olga, does not detract anything from the *reality* of her existence. She has had, in fact, the same *need* to be Lina in order to endure her wedding.

There is no identity that does not represent some kind of mediation between what we *feel* we are and what we *should* be. The ideas that gradually we have of ourselves are not born *in* the vacuum of our minds, but *from* the constant relationship with others. In the case of Francis or of Olga, the confirmation of what they feel they are doesn't come from men but from out-of-body and divine entities, which they can't escape.

After all, in our imagination, there has always been this idea of being able to be someone *else* from who we seem to be. The very idea of reincarnation, for example, shared by millions of human beings, confirms the hypothesis that our current identity can be ephemeral and tied to the current human and social context. Similarly, especially in Eastern cultures, ample space is given to the human possibility of reaching a state of enlightenment, called *satori*, in which our consciousness grasps the inner meaning and the unspeakable nature of all things.

Something like that happened to Francis and happens to Olga.

Something from where she can't come back even if she wanted to. Which is not to say that she can't lead a *normal* life, taking on a role in the shared reality, but simply that she can *never* go back to *being* Lina, just like Francis did not return to his family and his social identity.

Becoming aware of self, in its disturbing or enchanted aspects, is a prerogative of the experience of *hearing voices*. It arises from the *dialogue* and the daily *interaction* with them. The *voices* guide us to the knowledge of ourselves and of the world and *reveal* the secret purpose of our existence.

It is not something new to us. The *voice* of our parents, of our priest, of our teacher... had the same action on our mind. It taught us to recognize ourselves as children, students, believers... and it gave us the coordinates to move in the world and recognize common language and common logic as *ours*. The only difference is that in this case the *dialogue* takes place with *voices* that do not belong to reality as we have inherited it from our parents.

Since we can't shut them up, we might as well have a *dialogue* with them. And this is the suggestion that we took from the *voice hearers* of ROMME. The *dialogue* will not always be easy, it will often unsettle us, sometimes it will terrify us, and some other times it will make us tremble with emotion, but if we get to the end of this path, probably, our consciousness and perception will gain skills and capabilities that were previously unknown.

But is this doable? How?

This question can only be answered starting from the concrete experiences of those who hear *voices*. I will mention, among others, the statements of three women, different from each other, who were able to have a *dialogue* with the voices and make this dialogue a tool for individual and collective growth. A mystic, St. Teresa of Avila; a representative of the new age,

Eillen Caddy; a free researcher, Emy.

All these three women have been able to find the *key* to start a selection and a dialogue with the *voices*. Teresa was aided by the religious tradition that, more than any other one, has developed strategies for understanding and managing the *voices*; Eillen was supported by the new age philosophy that says that everyone is or can be a *channel* for the transmission of divine messages; Emy, instead, the only one to have had an experience of psychiatric therapy, is still searching for a meaning to the experience, and uses in an eclectic way the knowledge acquired from telepathic studies or the Rosicrucian philosophy, to collocate philosophically what happens to her.

All three have been able to manage a positive *dialogue* with their *voices*, recognizing their identity and building, from this dialogue, their daily existence. The case of Eillen, furthermore, is particular because the *voice* that has been her guide for her entire life, has become the *guide* of hundreds of other people who did not hear it but did recognize its meaning and moral authority.

But let's examine their statements. Teresa of Avila writes:

"So, while I considered why your justice refuses to so many of your faithful servants the favours and graces that I received, despite my unworthiness, You answered me: "You serve me, and don't think about anything else." It was the first time that I heard from You, and I was very scared." (Teresa D'AVILA 1985, p. 183)

Thus the story of the relationship of Teresa with the voice of God that will accompany her all her life begins. We often like to think of the saints as extra-ordinary people who are able to manage their own experiences in a way that is radically different from our way. In reality they experience the same anxieties and fears in the face of what happens to them. The words of Teresa are unequivocal:

"I would also like to make myself be understood because it is still at the beginning, so when the Lord grants these favours, the soul does not understand them and does not know what to do. Pain is the greatest then if God leads the soul to the path of fear as He did with me, and the soul doesn't find anybody that understands, while it would be a vivid joy if someone did a faithful picture of her condition, in order to be able to see by herself the path that she is on, being useful in any degree of prayer to know what needs to be done. If I have suffered a lot and I have wasted a lot of time, it was precisely for not knowing what I had to do." (Teresa D'AVILA 1985, p. 144)

The problems of Teresa are not, as you can see, different from those of every human being who begins to *hear voices*. Her first reaction is the fear of being in the grip of illusion, or worse, a victim of the devil. Her first omission is to try and remain silent to avoid the judgment of others.

"As I talked to a person whom I had met recently, the Lord deigned to admonish me; and He lit up my great blindness, he made me understand that these friendships were not appropriate to me.

Jesus Christ presented very stern, letting me know how disappointed He was. I saw Him with the eyes of the soul, but more clearly than with those of the body, and He made such a lasting impression on me that, despite twenty-six years went by, I can still see Him. I was so frightened and confused that I did not want to see anymore the person with whom I was talking.

I did not know that one could see other than with the eyes of the body. And this penalized me because the devil, keeping me in this opinion, made me believe that it was impossible, that it was an illusion, a trick of Satan and other things like that, even though deep down I remained under the impression that it was the work of God, and not a deception. But as this thought I did not want to genius, I tried it myself to see an illusion, looking from a word to anyone." (Teresa D'AVILA 1985, p. 83)

Moreover the people who Teresa turns to for help, despite being confessors of great sensitivity and religious vocation, do not seem to understand her experience, obsessed as they are to rule out the presence of the devil in any extra/*ordinary* manifestation hitting humans. Their attitude is similar to that of modern psychiatrists and psychotherapists who classify the human behaviour and experiences without being able to understand them and hear them in their depth and reality. About confessors and psychiatrists of every age and place, Teresa writes:

"As for me, I am more afraid of those who are very afraid of the devil than of the devil himself, because he can do no harm to me, while those, especially if they are confessors, can throw the soul into fear: because of them I spent several years in such serious troubles that I still marvel that I was able to bear them." (Teresa D'AVILA 1985, p. 250)

How can you blame her. The suggestions and recommendations of these confessors were remarkably similar to the things that are told to the lay *voice hearers* who are locked up in psychiatric wards around the world. Teresa is not allowed to read and meditate in isolation, she must reject the messages she receives and consider them manifestations of the devil. Even she is prescribed to make the sign of the cross and make the sign of the horns[1] at every hint of extrasensory vision. And,

---

[1] *Note of the Translator:* "Its earliest use can be seen in India, as a gesture very commonly used by Gautama Buddha as Karana Mudra which is synonymous with expulsion of demons and removal of obstacles like sickness or negative thoughts. The same usage can be seen in Italy and Mediterranean culture as well where, when confronted with unfortunate events, or simply when these events are mentioned, the sign of the horns may be given to ward off bad luck. It is also used traditionally to counter or ward off the "evil eye" (*malocchio*). With fingers down, it is a common apotropaic gesture, by which superstitious people seek protection in unlucky situations (It is a more Mediterranean equivalent of knocking on wood). [...]"
(http://en.wikipedia.org/wiki/Sign_of_the_horns)

first of all, she should not talk about it with anyone.

"Once a confessor I turned to from the beginning given that he was a good soul, advised me not to say anything to anybody, as silence would now be better.

I didn't mind such advice, because in manifesting these things to the confessor I felt so much repugnance and shame as I would not have felt while confessing the biggest sins; and this especially when the graces were greater, because I felt I was not being believed and that they would mock me. I wanted to keep silent also because I was afraid that for this the reverence I owed to God's graces would be affected." (Teresa D'AVILA 1985, p. 253)

And more:

"Many servants of God, whom I rightly thought highly of, had gathered to deal with my matters. I only talked with one of them, and I just talked with others when he told me. Furthermore they cared about me and, fearing that I was deluded by the devil, they discussed gravely to come to my aid. (...)

My confessor came to me, therefore, to say that these fellows (I think they were five or six, and all great servants of God) had agreed to declare myself to be victim of the devil, so I did not have to take communion so often, but I had to distract myself and never be alone." (Teresa of AVILA 1985, p. 245)

As with every other human being who hears voices, regardless if they are dictated by the devil or from *mental illness*, for Teresa the measures that tend to limit her freedom of choice and communication spring into action.

"Since a few days earlier they had taken away from me the communion and prohibited loneliness, the only things that were comforting me, and I didn't have anybody with which to talk,

because everyone was against me. When I spoke of my pain, some laughed at me as if I was delusional, others warned my confessor to be on guard and others said clearly that I was at the mercy of the devil." (Teresa of AVILA 1985, p. 246)

Teresa obeys the instructions she receives, albeit with suffering and without obtaining any benefit. In her culture and education, as well as in the culture of each of us, the deep-seated idea is that there are *others* who can clarify what happens to us better than we can. Experts of the human and superhuman things and experiences.

"Those were erudite and their life was incomparably more holy than mine: why not believing then?" (Teresa of AVILA 1985, p. 246) says the holy woman rhetorically. Her experience, like that of many voice hearers, shows that it is essential to find a cultural context or a guide to learn how to decipher and how to have a *dialogue* with the voices. None of those who do *not* hear them or do *not* believe in their reality can be of any help. This is true especially for those who, invested with a certain authority and power, try to impose silence upon them.

The *voice* of God becomes for Teresa the guide for her to learn how to listen, recognize and communicate with her. In this *listening* Teresa takes advantage of the experience of other saints of the church and of a *reliable* method of discernment developed by them.

Teresa writes:

"When I began to read the 'Confessions of St. Augustine' I thought I saw my life in them, and commended myself very much to this glorious saint.

When I got to his conversion and read about the voice he heard in the garden, I had such a vivid impression of it as if I was hearing it too, and for a long time I kept melting in tears, my soul tormented by tremendous struggle." (Teresa of AVILA

1985, p. 103)

Getting in touch and learning about the experiences of others who *hear* or have heard *voices*, apart from the substantial differences that may exist in the stories of each one, is a fundamental step in building a positive relationship with the *voices* themselves. At least because it decreases the anxiety we feel in front of them and it shows us a concrete possibility to manage them. This alone is not enough, but it is certainly important to be able to draw from the knowledge of others who have had the same experience, in order to find one's bearings within it. The experience of others helps us not to suffer the *voices* passively, but to relate to them *discerning* what we do or don't consider compatible with our existence and our morals.

In Teresa's case, her main issue was whether that *who* spoke to her was really the Christ or, instead, the devil trying to steal her soul. With regards to this, her confessors did not seem to be able to help. Obsessed as they were by what they could not explain, their only action was to ban this or that religious practice, hoping to prevent the *voice* to take possession of the mind of their protégé.

Here, as we have already seen in the relationship between psychiatrists and patients, confessors engage in a furious battle with the *voice*, to obtain control over Teresa.

"When the Lord gave me a command in prayer and the confessor imposed another one on me, His Majesty would come back to tell me to follow the word of the confessor. Then He would make him change his mind, causing him to give me the same command." (Teresa D'AVILA 1985 p. 254)

In the face of this *impossible* tug of war between the confessors and the *voice*, the only relief came to Teresa from the latter.

"When it was forbidden to read many books in vernacular I was very displeased because some of them lifted me up a lot, and I

could no longer read because the permitted ones were in Latin. But the Lord said to me: "Do not worry because I will give you a living book" (Teresa D'AVILA 1985, p. 254)

As you can see the *voices* acquire value and meaning also, and especially with regards to the senseless overreaction that they cause in our interlocutors. As HEIDEGGER would say, it seems that what saves us is born right there where there is a danger, what worries us seems to be the only thing that calms us. Just as Teresa writes:

"... these words sufficed to take away my anguish and calm me completely: "Do not be afraid my child, it's me, and I will not abandon you. Do not be afraid!"

In the state I was in, no one would be able to calm me down, or at least it seemed to me that it would take many hours. But with just those words I immediately felt peaceful, full of courage, strength, confidence and light." (Teresa D'AVILA 1985, p. 247-248)

After all, the only real source of anxiety for Teresa was not represented by *hearing voices*, but by the uncertainty of whether or not to consider it a divine *gift* or a demonic *temptation*. The religious culture recognizes the existence of an invisible and superhuman world and, above all, it recognizes as *possible* that this can come into contact with us or, better, with *some* of us. The fact that they are not perceived by others or that they can't be recorded by our instruments, for the religious is not proof of the inexistence of the *voices*, but rather of their supernatural nature. The fact that they are perceived by a few, furthermore, is an integral part of the mystery that surrounds the plan of God for every man. In other words, the divine nature of these communications is confirmed by the same *evidence* that make psychiatrists say with certainty that one is faced with a *mental illness*.

In fact I think there is only one apparent conflict between these two positions. If we substitute the word *devil* to the more scientific, but just as random word *mental illness*, we find that psychiatry does nothing but continuing the long tradition of denial that starts with Teresa's confessors, goes through the Courts of the Holy Inquisition to come to the modern psychiatric wards. What appears to us as a scientific fact is rather direct legacy of the eternal fear and the universal struggle to deny *evil*. Where by *evil* I mean not only the individual and collective unease or suffering, but also the possibility that people *sin*, that is, they do not comply with the order that we have given ourselves with their thoughts, words and deeds. Catholics have always Satan up, rather than men, to answer for this blasphemous choice. Similarly psychiatry has up *mental illness* to answer for this, rather than the people who act, think and speak in a way that they *shouldn't*. In either case, to *punish* Satan or *treat* mental illness confessors as well as psychiatrists act on the bodies and minds of the people who are *inhabited* by them. Irresponsible in theory, in practice treated as the worst criminals or the most infectious plague.

But let's go back to Teresa. What did she hear? And how did she manage to convince herself of the divine source of her experience?

We talked about *discernment*. It is a basically simple process that leads the *voice hearer* to verify the correspondence of the messages she receives with the cultural or personal framework that the *voice* itself has provided. In this case, with the Holy Scriptures. If a *voice* claims to be God, its communications must conform to what is written on the Holy Scriptures. Teresa takes this point of view from this exhortation of St. Vincent Ferrer to Christian mystics:

"If they tell you things against the faith, the Sacred Scripture and the good morals, and they support their doctrine with the prestige of supernatural events, you scorn their visions as a result of dementia and their raptures as rage." (Cit. in Teresa

D'AVILA 1985, p. 199)

The method is the only one available to us in front of divine, demonic and human *voices* as well. The complications arise from that sometimes high percentage of discretion that we have to interpret the events, and that sometimes can be guided more by our fears and our needs than by common sense. There is in fact no cultural context that doesn't present discrepancies and contradictions, also very deep ones. For example, when we *discern* about the divine nature of certain communications we receive from a voice that claims to be God, we can refer to various arguments of the Scriptures that deal with this matter and, in particular, to the philosophy of the Old or the New Testament.

Carmelo is in the criminally insane hospital because he is accused of setting fire to his mother's house in order to purify the demonic presences that lived there. Bettino did the same thing. They were convinced by the suggestions of their *voices* when the vengeful and relentless God of the Old Testament invested them with this purifying task. After all, wasn't it the same *voice* of God that led Abraham to the point of killing his son Isaac to prove his faith or that spoke to Noah to reveal the approaching end of the world through the flood?

This God, whom we truly believe we have replaced with the merciful God of the New Testament, still *speaks* to people and produces most of the disasters that we ascribe to the *voices*. It's the God who speaks to the moralists of every age, to those who make of intolerance their flag, to those who have managed or run concentration camps or mental asylums, to those who set fire to the homeless on the street or kill the prostitutes. It is not necessary that they *hear* that voice. Often they have it inside: it is their own conscience.

When I talk about *discernment*, I believe that we must learn to also *discern* between the *voices* who claim to be divine, and the ones that are so, both when they speak to Teresa of AVILA and when they set Carmelo's heart on fire. An example of what I mean is given by Jesus Christ in his response to the temptations of Satan. We read in the Gospel of Matthew:

"Then Jesus was led up by the Spirit into the wilderness to be tempted by the devil. And when he had fasted forty days and forty nights, he afterward hungered.

And the tempter came and said unto him: 'If thou art the Son of God, command that these stones become bread'. *But he answered and said:* 'It is written, Man shall not live by bread alone, but by every word that proceedeth out of the mouth of God'.

Then the devil taketh him into the holy city; and he set him on the pinnacle of the temple, and saith unto him: 'If thou art the Son of God, cast thyself down, for it is written, He shall give his angels charge concerning thee: and, on their hands they shall bear thee up, lest haply thou dash thy foot against a stone'.

Jesus said unto him: 'Again it is written, Thou shalt not make trial of the Lord thy God'.

Again, the devil taketh him unto an exceeding high mountain, and showeth him all the kingdoms of the world, and the glory of them; and he said unto him: 'All these things will I give thee, if thou wilt fall down and worship me.' *Then saith Jesus unto him:* 'Get thee hence, Satan: for it is written, Thou shalt worship the Lord thy God, and him only shalt thou serve'.

Then the devil leaveth him; and behold, angels came and ministered unto him.

As we see Christ responds to each temptation by placing each response in the path of the religious tradition. He *chooses* from a range of possible principles, some endorsed by Satan himself, those that allow him to respond meaningfully to the provocations he receives. There is no rejection of *dialogue*, nor denial of the reality of the interlocutor; there is a tight argument that allows him to overcome the impasse in which the other tries to catch him.

The same Christ's technique is used by Teresa and all the mystics who have gone and go through the history of the world. It is a technique, but also and above all, an art that is revealed only to those who have the time, the ability and perseverance to work at it in an attempt to take control of it. The failures in this challenge are a common occurrence, exacerbated by a social and human environment that is, today, more than ever hostile towards those who try to master this experience.

Teresa writes

"I would also like to make myself understood because it is still early times, so when the Lord grants these graces, the soul does not understand and does not know what to do. The greatest pain then is if God leads her through the path of fear as he did with me, and she doesn't find anybody who understands, while she would experience vivid joy if one gave a faithful picture of her condition, in order to be able to see herself the path that she is beating, being useful to know, in any degree of prayer, what needs to be done. If I have suffered a lot and I have wasted a lot of time, it was precisely because of not knowing what I had to do." (Teresa of AVILA 1985, p. 144)

The *voice* of God comes to her assistance:

"One day, after having lasted a long time in prayer and begged the Lord to help me please him, I began the recitation of the hymn, and while I was reciting, rapture took me so sudden I was almost left beside myself. It was the first time that God granted me this grace, and I could never doubt it for it was very obvious. I then heard these words: I do not want you to

converse with men anymore, but only with angels." (Teresa D'AVILA 1985, p. 236)

Since that time, always referring firmly to the Scriptures, Teresa begins to have a *dialogue* with God and to recognize him. Starting from her experience, she outlines the key features of what is happening to her. Her reflections about the nature and effects of *hearing voices* are relevant more than ever and consistent with the auditory experiences, both mystical and secular, of the other voice hearers. Teresa writes, in fact:

"I would like to show the illusions for which it is easy to fall. It is true that those who have experience won't fall or will fall very rarely for them, but it is required that the experience is extensive.

I would also like to show the difference there is when words come from the good spirit and when from the bad one and say at the same time that they can be a concern of the intellect, or words that our own spirit directs to itself. I do not know if this is possible, but until now it seemed so to me." (Teresa of AVILA 1985, p. 238)

And then she goes on to analyze:

"When one takes one's time to recommend to God with great imploration a deal that worries her, it is very easy at times that she feels like she is hearing his answer, whether the question for which she prays will be answered or not. But those who have heard what the words of God sound like see what it is, because the difference is huge.

Likewise if it is the intellect, because, even though it is clever, one sees at once who that is: he who composes and speaks, while it is very different to compose a speech and to hear it from others. Even the intellect realizes that, instead of listening, he is talking. In addition, his words are like a dull and fantastic sound, missing the clarity that is characteristic of God's words, without saying that we can suspend the speech and be silent, while this is impossible with God's words.

Another more obvious sign is that the words of the intellect do not produce anything, while those of God are words and deeds. Even though they are not words of devotion, but only of reprimand, they change in an instant the soul's disposition: they enable it, enlighten it, soften it, shower it with joy, and if it is in the aridity, in restlessness and anxiety, it feels like a hand that takes away all of its sufferings, or something better. - Well, it seems that God wants to make it clear that He is powerful and that his words are deeds." (Teresa of AVILA 1985, p. 239)

The words that come from the *voice* of God

"... are very distinct: one does not hear them with the ears of the body, but they are heard much more clearly than if they were perceived with them, so that any efforts against this would not succeed at all. At least among us, if you do not want to pay heed to some, you plug your ears or attend to something else in such a way that, while hearing, you would not listen, but here that is impossible. You must listen even if you do not want to: it's as if the intellect is forced to pay attention to what the Lord wants it to understand. Wanting or not wanting is not relevant: That who can do everything takes over, persuading us that there is no option but doing as He wants. And I know it from experience, because with my fears I tried to resist for nearly two years. Sometimes I still try, but there's little benefit." (Teresa of AVILA 1985, p. 238)

"Often I happened to hesitate quite a lot before I could believe what I was hearing, fearing I was the victim of some delusion: but, this, after everything was over, because in the midst of the act of grace doubt is impossible. Then, after a long time I would see all things come true.

The words of God are fixed in the mind so well that one can't forget them, while those of the intellect are like a flash of thought that soon wears off." (Teresa of AVILA 1985, p. 241)

The words that come from Satan, instead,

"... not only do not leave good effects, but they produce unpleasant ones. I've heard those no more than two or three times, but the Lord has always made me figure out whose words they were. (...)

The words of the devil do not produce any affection, but disgust and fear." (Teresa D'AVILA 1985, p. 243-244)

As we can see, the life of the mystics is not as straightforward as it seems. They doubt their mental health, the nature of their experiences, the truth of what they hear, doubt that they have been chosen, doubt that they are worthy of it. The path through which they accept their fate is long and tortuous, and they often fail to get to the end of it, they lose themselves irremediably along the platforms of some train station.

The religious mystics, among the voice hearers, are those that have the easiest life. They are expected to have *visions*, to come into contact in some way with the invisible world that governs our reality. They have a very stable cultural context of reference, built through the experience of generations of ascetics and researchers of the spirit and, above all, that is socially tolerated. The only thing that is asked of them is to restrict the places and modalities of their communications. The fasting of St. Catherine of Siena, for example, is a divine gift or a miracle as long as it has the convent as a material and symbolic frame; it turns into *anorexia* if practiced in a studio or an apartment of any of our cities.

What mystics do, seems to be the *repetition* of an already written script. They rarely add anything new to the experience in which they are involved. Instead, they follow the instructions of their spiritual fathers as the sailors follow the compass or the stars. Their experience makes sense as long as it moves in the footsteps of tradition. Without this continuity, and these cardinal points, they risk losing themselves and not coming back.

The situation is different for the laypersons who meet the *voices*. They have to define a path and build themselves a cultural context of reference; defend themselves from the accusation of being *ill* and avoid hospitalization; find a socially acceptable way to express and communicate their experience and to realise it.

As Teresa says, God's words are deeds. This of course applies to any *voice* we hear. If they speak to us, it is in order to achieve a purpose which can be internal, social, or, on occasion, universal. We *must* understand who we really are; we *must* create a refuge for the angels; we *must* restore the heart of the planet.

Every time they open the communication channel, the *voices* do it to remind us of our *impossible* mission or our commitment to ourselves. With more or less capacity to understand, depending on the nature and type of relationship we have built with her, the *voice* is always there in the foreground to affirm the centrality of her reasoning. Often the *voice hearers* claim to have acted as requested, with the secret hope that then it would stop tormenting them. Acting like that is never a good strategy, although sometimes it can have positive and unhoped-for results. Better, if we can, to establish a *dialogue* and to engage the *voices* in a heated debate with our own reality of human beings.

If the *impossible* seems to be their plan, it is up to us to make it *possible*. The *dialogue* I'm thinking of is a constant work of translation to *practice* of the received messages. That does not mean to uncritically realize the suggestions, but indeed to make them practical, weighing them against the every-day reality, our feelings, our personal relationships, our ideas.

Often the *dialogue* with the voices retraces the steps of what might be called a path of initiation. They constantly put us to the test and, at the same time, they provide us with tangible evidence of the *truth* of what they state. As we know, every serious *initiation* leads, sooner or later, to a real *leap of faith*, a time when the initiate is asked for the *impossible*, with the aim to move his consciousness, in a definitive way, to another life state. Only this experience, in which the adept renounces definitely his/her own will, consciousness and individuality to indulge in the unknown, marks his/her passage to another dimension of being. It is, in all senses, an experience of no return. In it the initiate defies his/her physical and mental death to become *other* than him/herself, or to be who he/she *is*.

So it should not surprise us too much, if the *voice* he is hearing is suggesting to George the ultimate test: getting through the wall of *reality* with his bus. It is no less *sensible* than the Don Juan's *voice* that accompanies Carlos Castaneda in his leap into the void of a ravine in the Mexican Plateau. Even here, it makes no substantial difference to be *guided* by the voice of a material or invisible person. What really matters is the type of relationship that we have with this.

Moreover, on closer view, men have always put themselves at risk in order to achieve some definitive knowledge about the nature of things. It really seems that only where there is a danger, that which saves can be born. Many of us give up understanding, others *can't* understand.

There is no rational or scientific recipe that can make us distinguish a true master or spiritual guide, from an incompetent who needlessly put our lives at risk. This is true in the material world as well as in the invisible world of the *voices*.

The fact that the *voices* are spiritual does not mean that they can't be *false* or *meaningless*. There is no reason to believe their word for it, nor can they have any authority other than the one we allow them to have. For this reason I emphasize *dialogue*: it is the only tool we have to explore and verify this experience. By the way: the *voices* that do not agree to have a dialogue with us are to be considered, in all likelihood, unproductive and even harmful to our inner growth. *Dialogue* is another *selection* criterion for hearing that I would suggest.

The story of Eillen Caddy is, indeed, emblematic of this.

Today Eillen is a dynamic older woman, co-founder of the Findhorn community in northern Scotland. An ordinary community, like other ones that were created in various parts of the world in the 70s, but with an *extra*ordinary story behind it.

For years, the Community has been governed by the messages a *voice* communicated to Eillen. The same *voice*, moreover, had changed her life and given rise to the community.

The first contact between Eillen and the *voice* that reveals to her it's God, takes place in a chapel dedicated to prayer and meditation. Eillen had just left her husband, abandoned her children and had fallen in love with another man. In a short time she had altered her social and personal identity in a radical way, discovering resources and sensations that she had never thought of having. This attracted and worried her at the same time.

Eillen writes about that first experience:

"From the bottom of my heart I cried for help: I did not have anybody other than God to turn to.

<Be quiet and know that I am God>

The voice was perfectly clear, and I turned to see who had spoken. It could not be Peter and Sheena, and there was no one else in the room. The voice was in my head. I was going crazy? I sat still, rigid with fear, my eyes narrowed." (Eillen CADDY 1993, p. 32)

We are in the twentieth century; Teresa's fear of being tempted by the devil is replaced by Eillen's fear of going insane or being already mad. It's the first sensible knee-jerk reaction that you can expect from those who live in a reality that excludes from its horizon everything that is not seen, heard or recorded.

"The voice continued:

<You made a very serious decision in your life. But if you follow My voice, everything will be fine. I made you and Peter meet for a very special purpose, to do a specific job for Me. You will work as one, and you will realize this more fully as time goes by. Only a few have been guided in this way. Do not be afraid, because I am with you>" (Eillen CADDY 1993, p. 32)

The voice seems to understand Eillen's discomfort. As one who deeply understands human beings, has always spoken with them and has created them, God's *voice* calms her and at the same time provides the first indications of the meaning to be given to this experience.

JAYNES would say that the right brain, triggered by the stress of having to make a series of important decisions for her own life, regained control over Eillen's left hemisphere and consciousness, speaking to her through the *voice* of God. Perhaps, but the task that this *voice* will put into Eillen's hands only partly coincides with the resolution of her problems. Above all it will open extraordinary collective perspectives that are, in no way, closed in her skull or in her caravan.

"When we left the chapel, I said, trembling:

<I had a strange, terrible experience in there. I heard a voice speaking to me, and it was inside of me. I'm afraid I'm going crazy>" (Eillen CADDY 1993, p. 32).

Eillen can't keep all that fear for herself. She knows that if she tells what happened, it is likely that her friends will confirm her insanity, but she can't do otherwise. Peter, the man she is in love with, and Sheena, his wife, on the other hand have an unexpected reaction.

"<It's magnificent, Eillen! - was the reaction of Sheena when I had finished speaking – It's the confirmation of everything. Now I'm sure that it was God that brought together you and Peter>

I was struck: for me there was nothing to cheer about.

<Repeat the words that you have heard> Peter urged.

< Be quiet and know that I am God - I repeated slowly - I recognize these words. I read them somewhere in the Bible>

Already in this first experience, as well as the *reasonable* doubts of the case, there are all the elements that will bring Eillen to learn to listen and have a dialogue with her *voice*. There is a human and cultural context that welcomes and recognizes this as a *real* experience. People who recognise a value and a sense in what is happening to her. And there is an instinctive *discernment* that enables Eillen to recognize the divine origin of the message.

But we are only at the beginning of the *dialogue*, when the auditory experience is only a *monologue* and there is a risk it will remain so.

"Peter and Sheena were convinced that I had really heard the voice of God. I was not at all sure, but if I accepted what I had heard, it had to be the voice of God. The more I thought about it the more I felt worried. I remembered the people with whom

God speaks in the Bible, but those were very special, with special tasks to complete. Why did god have to talk to a woman who had left her husband and children to 'live in sin' with another man?" (Eillen CADDY 1993, pp. 32-33)

Reasonable doubts the ones Eillen had, which did not take into account then, and perhaps could not do it since the emotional impact of these events that involved her, the fact that God works in mysterious ways. At that moment, after all, the only thing that was really needed was to close in some way the gap that was open *in* her head in order to keep out that *voice* that invaded her.

Resistance to the divine will is a constant in the relationship between God and men. Not everyone likes to become a saint, if only because sanctity exposes us to martyrdom, confusion and misunderstanding. The divine catapults us beyond the human and historical reality in which we live; it cuts our ties with the world of affections and desires; it destroys our history, our individuality and our identity. It eradicates us, so to speak, from the world of the majority, forcing us into the *desert* of truth.

Of course it is not always the case, but the risk of becoming saints and, therefore, statues, idols, holy pictures and souvenirs, is always present in every mystical experience. What is striking about Teresa or Eillen is that, although touched by the divine *voice*, they still assert their human identity and character. Probably the stories of the saints and mystics should be *read* from their own point of view, rather than *told* by others.

Despite having met in that little church the *voice* of the God that will accompany her throughout her life, offering comfort and joy, Eillen describes this period as

"... the most terrifying of my life." (Eillen CADDY 1993, p. 33)

It is basically the period in which everyone stands a chance to understand, have a dialogue and learn to manage the *voices*.

Throughout this period Eillen had always Peter and Sheena close to her. They firmly believed in the possibility that each of us may become a conscious *channel* of the messages and energy coming from higher beings. So, listening and selecting the *voices* becomes a primary instrument of knowledge of the true nature of the universe. A bit like, in the Catholic religion, the Marian *visions* become messages and operational instructions for people.

The listening method that they *imposed* upon Eillen was very hard, but it certainly served to temper her will and prepare her psychologically to do it alone.

"During this period of my apprenticeship, I had to take the time to listen to the inner voice three times a day: at 6 am, noon and 9 pm." (Eillen CADDY 1993, p. 37)

To the *voice hearers* who read this statement it may sound impossible to limit the *dialogue* with the voices to such a rigid time and manner. The *voices* for the most part speak and behave in complete anarchy, not taking into any account our mental state, where we are or our desire to hear them. This, at least, is the experience of those who have little control over them.

There are experiences, like Eillen's ones, where the perseverance, with which consistent and clear rules of relationship are imposed to oneself and to the *voices*, leads progressively to a reduction of the feeling of interference and invasion they cause in our lives, while allowing some form of constructive *dialogue*.

The message that is communicated to the *voices* is of this sort: now I can't pay attention to you. I recognize that what you have to say is important and complex and requires all my attention. We will talk later, in peace and for as long as it takes.

This communication strategy has allowed several people I know to give some *order* to this experience. Not only that. By doing so they were able to find some form of mediation between *listening* to the *voices* and to the people around us.

If the story of Antonio and St. Philip so often ends in a psychiatric clinic, this is mainly due to the fact that Antonio can't in any way mediate between the *duty* of listening to both his wife and St. Philip. However the problem does not lie entirely *in* Antonio. It's also true that often those who are around people who *hear voices* can't or do not know how to articulate any *meaningful* discourse. Like Teresa's confessors, whenever we open our mouth is to *forbid* Antonio to do something, to *deny* what he is saying, to *punish* him for something he did.

Part of the frankly destructive contents of the *voices* does not derive as much from their innate wickedness, as by the need to guard us against the danger that the good advice and the voices of our loved ones may convince us not to pay attention to them. Those who are the closest to us will be described as traitors and murderers; we will ourselves be portrayed as despicable beings that deserve every sort of disgrace and insult from the entire universe.

The method *imposed* on Eillen instead tended to select and build a shared habit of listening to the *voices*.

"At first I could hear many different voices and I was confused. Sheena told me to identify just the first I had heard at Glastonbury.

<Try to ignore all the other ones and focus on that: slowly you'll see that the other ones will disappear. That's why I want you to take note of everything that you hear, so I can help you

distinguish, until there will be no shadow of doubt as to which voice is that of God, and you will follow only that >" (Eillen CADDY 1993 , p. 37-38)

Writing and, therefore, the possibility of a thoughtful analysis of what we *hear*, frees from the emotional impact that the very fact of *hearing voices* causes; it is another fundamental method for anyone who wants to try to find and disentangle the thread of this matter. Among other things, it becomes an essential document to allow third parties to know and evaluate what we are hearing. The *voices* we hear are, in fact, *inaudible*. This handicap can be partly overcome by writing the content of what they say and compare it with others.

That's what the young woman from Catania does, for example, when she transcribes the messages transmitted by divine *voices* and then discusses them with her prayer group. To date, she has never felt, nor has she ever been judged *ill* by anybody. Not only that. By directing the hearing of *voices*, she has gained only comfort, knowledge and guidance from it, without challenging her existence in the social world of the majority.

There are hundreds of such experiences. As many as the experiences of people who can't get to the bottom of anything. ROMME's intuition is also true for us: we need to allow the people who *hear voices* to come out, meet and exchange their experiences. We, who don't hear them, just have to not interfere in this and, if we want, to lend them a discreet and respectful ear.

When this happens, stories like the ones of Eillen become the *norm*.

Whether by ourselves or with the help of others, it is essential to be able to select the *voices* that we listen to. Focusing on the one we consider the most consistent with our character and our expectations, is different from the suggestion to *ignore them* that comes from several perspectives. We must think of ourselves as a radio. Once turned on, we must find our *wavelength*. If we can't do it in a short time, someone may *sensibly* think of turning us off. It is what psychiatric therapy does, as we have seen.

The life of Eillen since then is *guided* by her inner voice that advises her on what to do in every circumstance. Gradually she learns to use it by herself. Without waiting for it to speak, Eillen asks the voice all sorts of advice and has a dialogue with it about the decisions she needs to take.

The trust placed by others in the messages that Eillen was receiving was so intense that it gave her the strength and courage to continue, even when they seemed frankly foolish and provocative. With God's *guidance* Eillen and Peter, after various vicissitudes, founded the Findhorn community in a place designated by the *voice*. A desert and unproductive place where they arrived without any resource and any idea of what was expected of them.

The community grew, thanks to the instructions of Eillen's inner *voice* and the help of other *voices* and natural *entities* who taught them how to communicate with the *devas*, the spirits of the plants. They themselves gave recommendation to human beings about where, how, when and what to do to make the harvest more prosperous. With these *guides* they made that land become fertile and productive, building an experience that is now well-established and extended to several hundred residents.

This is the mission that God had given her: to create a place where the visible and invisible, matter and spirit, finite and infinite could meet. A *place of power*, as Don Juan would call it. A gap, a point of passage...

Today, the *voice* of Eillen has ceased to *guide* the community. I can imagine that it will continue its *mission* with Eillen, trying to prepare and guide her on the journey through death to Him.

Maybe the *voices* are just a biochemical imbalance in the brain, but what they allow us to do, think and understand is of such an awesome power and wonder, that it is necessary to fight so that they will never get *cured*. What is at stake is not just the besieged brain or the lives of those who *hear voices*; it's at stake the ability to remain sensible human beings in a world that still means something.

We should certainly learn to silence the cruel *voices* that persecute us, as well as we need to stop having nightmares at night. But as we would not accept to stop dreaming in order to *heal* from the illness of having nightmares, so we can't stop *hearing voices* to *heal* from the silly words that sometimes they yell at us.

Emy has found a personal and instinctive way to do it. Not a lonely path, and most importantly a way that is accessible to everybody.

As I write this *voices listening handbook*, I always have the fear of making, myself too, the mistake of sanctifying the people I'm talking about, preventing the healthy identification that can serve, I believe, to overcome isolation and fear of what is happening to us. Beyond the emphasis I put in what I write, I want to clarify that none of the people I have talked about so far, including Emy, is in itself less than *ordinary*. What's *extra*ordinary is the experience in which they are involved, the resources and the human possibilities it stimulates, the transformations it generates. If we try to put ourselves for a moment in Eillen's or Teresa's shoes, as well as Anthony's, I do not think we would have less doubts and less certainties of those they have had themselves. They are *ordinary* human beings who use *ordinary* tools that are made available by our culture.

The only real difference between Eillen CADDY and Carmelo,

the guy who was locked up in the criminally insane asylum for burning that house, is not *in* either of the two, let alone in the *voice* they heard (in both cases the *voice* of God), but *in* the human context around them. Where Eillen could compare and analyze her experience collectively, Carmelo remained homebound for days without speaking to anyone, leaving the fire flare up. Years of psychiatric therapy taught him to keep these *voices* to himself and to use liters of psychotropic drugs in liquid formulation to try and extinguish the fire. Paradoxically, the only thing they have *put out* has been his will. So Carmelo found himself helpless in the face of the imperative of God; powerless sure, but not so much that he couldn't light a match and sprinkle with alcohol the old clutter stacked in the attic.

We will come back to the question of risks, possibilities and limitations of psychopharmacological therapy in the management of the *voices*, if only because it is the choice of a significant number of those who use substances (legal or illegal they may be) to do it. For now, let's get into the experience of Emy as she tells it.

At one point, a voice said to me: "Why don't you heal yourself, you do so much for others and you don't heal yourself." I asked him what my illness was and the voice replied that I was dissociated. I asked him what it meant to him, the voice said that if I understood it, I could give a better explanation than the ones that are known.

I asked him to stay with me, help me, and that I would have tried to understand. So he did.

I asked him to come to me every day to talk and see if the next day I remembered the conversation. Thus began a mental dialogue that was conscious and logical. The dialogue went on for a while; then he told me to go to him. Here the trouble started; partly because I was afraid to deal with a voice that did disclose its name and that I did not know how to approach without the risk of humiliating myself. I was fully aware that if I had been disappointed, if I had been wrong, if the voice had been a hoax, I would have been plunged into the deepest despair.

In the meantime, I realized that it was not just a voice that I heard, they were numerous, I struggled to complete the commitment I had undertaken, because at one point there were many voices telling me, "Come to me" and I was starting again to be confused and afraid.

While I was having a telepathic dialogue I knew I had a real life, but in reality I did not remember my telepathic life.

So I realized about dissociation. There were no communicating vessels between the two realities. I told the voice this and he told me to write what we said telepathically to each other. I tried it, but when I would pick up the pen to write, my head was empty, I could not remember anything. Then I would drop the pen, I would go back to focus on my head and I would start to hear the voice again asking me if I had written, and I would reply that I could not. In telepathic life I was aware; it was in reality that I was dissociated.

I asked him to insist, I would tell him: "Now I'll pick up the pen, you keep calling me, yell, with your thought, let's see if I can hear." So he did, after a few days of practice I finally managed to write. Telepathy and writing had joined together. At this point some sentences related to the telepathic life would come out even in real dialogues.

Telepathic life and dialogues would join together.

At this point they asked me why I did not tell anybody the things I was told, either in reality or in my telepathic life. I told them that I did not know I had had a dialogue with different people and I had no memory anyway. The telepathic life for me was a fleeting moment, there remained no recollection. Then I asked them to get in three to talk to me at a distance of 10 minutes from each other and see if I remembered. So they did, but I could not remember anything. Then I asked them to tell each other what they told me and then, after 10 minutes, to ask me questions related to previous conversations. So they did, and I began to have vague memories. They were all committed to help me and all my requests were supported.

It was an exercise that lasted several months, at the same time. Then I realized that telepathy was linked to the setting. I would do it at home, at the office and in my car, never on the street. Then I asked them to help me, and when I was about to get off the car, I would tell them and ask to insist, to yell out loud with their thought. So telepathy was not related to the setting anymore, it was on every occasion and at all times. Paying attention would be sufficient.

I am a Province employee, I'm a union representative and I come down hard on my employer. The administration does not like me. At one point I met a Province politician that would want me in their circle. He introduced me to a prefect and a lawyer, he invited me to his parties, he wanted me to have fun and stop being in the union.

In fact he never mentioned my union activities, but at a time when I was associating with him, I went to the union meeting and a voice said to me "You have to choose: either the administration or the union!" Also I had a crush on someone and a voice said to me: "I don't care about your love, this is not what I wanted, I don't know what to do with it."

So this is how my head finally began to work seriously.

Since I was aware that I had no memory I asked other voices to remind me every day that that person was a bastard. And so they did. Every day a voice came to me and told me: "Look, that guy is a bastard!" A few days later I asked them why he *was a bastard and a voice said, "I don't know, you didn't tell why, you just asked us to remind you." Being logical and consistent, telepathic life and real life have reunited.*

At this point I was fully conscious and aware, and my subconscious was giving me back all the memories related to my mental life.

So I remembered that I had always heard the voices, since I was a girl, but I was in big trouble when I started to talk about it. I remembered all the times that the voices would push me to commit suicide, to be violent towards my children, to be malicious with colleagues and friends in order to keep me isolated and alone.

My situation seemed to me more or less normal. Separated, with two daughters, I was living in my own apartment; I was driving my car and I was working regularly in the office. My emotional life was very limited, both in friendships and in love. I did not want excitement; my commitment was to keep my balance. Moreover, I was always very tired, so I was happy to spend my free time sleeping. At some point, however, my heart began to feel dry and so I decided I had to do something. I was dissociated also because my real life was too limited and I was looking, in the telepathic dialogues, for the company that I did not have in reality.

When I realized in 1984/85 to hear "voices", they wanted to push me to deal drugs at school.

I, who have never used drugs, suddenly began to ask around what it was like to take drugs, where one could buy it, and more. It was this that caused me trouble. Until then I had never said a word about my thoughts. To start talking about it meant that I was "recomposing" myself. I did not have to talk about it, I think; I simply had to let these thoughts swirl around in my head and broadcast my thought among people whom I approached.

The "voices" began to push me to go out, I went to the disco, I didn't know the way well, I got there following the "voice". But I never got into any circle, either related to drugs or prostitution.

One evening a peremptory and persecutory voice, from which I could not escape, told me to give my daughter psychotropic drugs. She was two years old; she was shocked as I was. I said, "Okay, how much should I give her?" The voice said to me, "As much as you take." I answered yes. Then he said, "Now leave your daughter at your mother's and go out." So I did. I got into my car and started to go where I was told to go. I would say where I was by reading the road signs, and they were leading me. They told me to stop, to go into a bar, have a drink. So I did. Then I got back into the car and I left.

At one point I said, "In front of me there is a wall, do I have to turn right or left?" The voice began to shout "Push hard the accelerator, push, push, crash against that wall once and for all!"

The survival instinct has always had the upper hand. At that point I woke up, I was not annihilated, dazed, I was really lucid. I began to yell in my thought: "Fuck you, you go against that wall, you crash, you nasty bastard! I'm going home to my daughter."

I went home and off to bed. The next morning, the voice said to me, "How's your daughter?" "Well!" I replied. "What do you mean 'well', last night you gave her psychiatric drugs, she can't be well?!" "But yes," I replied, "She is well because I said I was going to give her the psychiatric drug, but actually I didn't give it to her." At that point he started to insult me and then he left saying "We will meet again!"

I could never tell this story to my husband, or to my family, because as I said about the voices, I was forced to take the psychiatric drugs. I lived in fear for so many years, without being able to stand up for myself, because I've never known against whom.

There were negative voices or, anyway, voices that bothered me. After reading some books of magic and esotericism, I began threatening to curse all those who bothered me and cursing, with all the anger and aggression I could express, the voices that wanted to hurt me. Something like, "May all the evil that you wish me, come back to you and hit you like a boomerang and break your heart" or "Damn you for eternity, bloody bastard!" or "May the curse and misfortune hit you and your family," with the addition of all the insults that came to my mind to vent my anger. In order for the curses to work, they must contain the power of our emotions.

In this way many negative voices have moved away, but I must always be alert. I have a vague impression that once you enter the astral world, it is not easy to get out, if not even impossible: to be there in a conscious way and being able to defend oneself, however, is less distressing.

While doing all this, there was a voice saying to me "You have to elevate your spirit." To do this I needed a religion to identify with. That's why I'm getting closer to "gnosis" which gives many explanations, both scientific and esoteric, on the problems of human beings, egos, astral travels and so on. Basically it is explaining to me how to define the experiences that I have had for years, involuntarily, instinctively and unconsciously. I asked if they consider the drug addicts trips a kind of astral travel, and I was told that we must not confuse the hallucinations with astral travel.

At this point I do not know if those who hear voices are like me, i.e. unaware psychics, or if they have hallucinations. When I started to talk about my voices many people wanted to convince me that they were hallucinations, but I was sure that they were instead thoughts coming from outside and they were *not a product of my mind, but I could not prove it.*

Now I'm sure that I was an unaware psychic, but I do not know what to say about others, my experience should apply to several people: this is the only way to confirm whether hallucinations and astral travels are quite separate things.

At one point, my dialogue with the voices became friendly. Because they were always there, I decided to use them to improve my life. When I didn't know what to do for dinner, I asked my thought, and suddenly an idea would come. Or, if I had to go shopping I would say: "Will you take note or shall I?" and the voice would say "I will" and at the supermarket he would tell me the list of what I needed. If I had a problem with my children I would say, "Listen, help me, I have this problem, what do you think about it?" Sometimes a dialogue would start, like between husband and wife, some other times I would hear the answer: "What is this, did you mistake me for your husband? I don't care about your problems." So I would respond telling him to fuck off, insulting him and pushing him away from me, because I am not interested in "shitheads", either in reality or in telepathy.

It is by really respecting the voices that I have become aware of the phenomenon and I can master it, as much as possible.

So, these are extensive excerpts of Emy's correspondence. In this story, a number of issues and knotty points that we have seen to be constitutive of the experience of *hearing voices* are explored and resolved. The recognition of the *reality* of the voices, their daily management, their evolutionary use, the need for a cultural context of reference... all topped off by the tenacity and vitality of this woman who has been able to turn that which for many becomes a disgrace, into a stroke of luck.

I left out, so far, Emy's reflections on the use of psychotropic drugs. Her experience in this regard is illuminating.

When the psychologist[2] administered the psychotropic drug to me, at first I tried Lexotan, but I couldn't tolerate it, it made me sleep. Then we went to Serenase associated with Akineton. At first I felt stoned and incapable of any reaction, concentration, clarity. I felt a little handicapped. Over time I got used to that new personality, rather flat, with no more imagination and creativity. It was very painful.

After a while, 6 months/1 year, I decided it wasn't that great, but I could manage to live even in that way; something had happened to me that I could not dominate on my own and, therefore, I needed the psychiatric drug until I would be strong enough to be able to dominate and control my anxieties, my troubles, and above all, the phenomenon of the "voices".

After I made that decision, I realized that I was tolerating the psychotropic drug much better than before. I found my concentration; I began to take on more responsibility than required in my role of administrative assistant, because I knew that if I could bear more responsibility I would become stronger.

I was elected to the School Board and discovered that it was the perfect place to release my aggression by putting up fights for what I believed. Then I began to take minutes during the meetings, re-discovering a terrific short-term memory. Everything helped to make me feel more alive, more real.

From time to time I would try to stop the psychiatric drug, but the phenomenon of the voices in a short time overwhelmed me, kept me from leading a normal life and I was forced to resume it.

I wanted to stop because I was missing too much my emotional, creative and sentimental life. I was cold, unfriendly and incapable of any passion or involvement. For my character

---

[2] (sic), Note of the Translator

it was like being impotent.

I took the psychotropic drug because I thought it would screen me, defend me from the phenomenon of the voices. In fact, the phenomenon has never ceased, it was only unconscious. By the time I was able to quit, my memory gave back to me my mental history that was a life that was parallel to real life. My conscious part was in reality, the unconscious was working at the same time, independently, leaving no trace. That was the dissociation.

Now that I'm putting myself back together and I do not use psychiatric drugs anymore, when I go to the disco I drink vodka or beer. Alcohol really is a screen. I feel a slight weight on my head, but it is closed, I do not hear voices and at the same time I feel like the armor in the body slowly dropped. Once the head is closed, the body is free: with the head open, the body is blocked. It's a defense, because if there is no control of the head, then I dominate the body, but if I can master the head, I set the body free.

There is, among those fighting to overcome the uses and abuses of psychiatry, a constant and accurate criticism of the compulsory administration of psychiatric drugs, based on the medical groundlessness of these "treatments" and on the undeniably devastating effects on the mind and body of those who take them. (see BREGGIN P. 1985; ANTONUCCI G. 1993; CESTARI R. 1994; ANTONUCCI G., Coppola A, 1995)

Then again one can't disagree with the testimony of Roberto, a former psychiatric patient, in one of the conventions on human rights:

"I wanted to say something about psychotropic drugs. They gave them to me in very high doses. When they gave me those drugs, I completely lost consciousness. A feature of these drugs is just to take away the capacity to express... to be critical towards reality. This is a bad thing because a person has a

meaning, and acquires a meaning, insofar as he or she is able to take a critical and highly critical attitude towards reality.

The psychotropic drugs take away this critical view of reality. And this is one reason why the drugs should be eliminated and abolished".

Psychotropic drugs are substances that alter the state of consciousness and perception of the people who take them. The problem is not so much, or only, to determine *whether* and to what extent they are harmful to the organism, but also, and above all, to understand whether the changes that they cause are the ones their users search at that particular time.

The equation psychotropic drugs = cure = illness is a psychiatric hoax. In fact, these drugs do not *cure* anything (nor they show, as psychiatrists would like, that there is a pathology underlying unacceptable behaviour). They in most cases *limit* people's judgment, criticism and action skills, producing a state of mental dependence and relational passivity which, paradoxically, can be experienced by people, given certain conditions, such as a relief. A bit like vodka sets Emy's body free, in the same way, sometimes, taking psychotropic drugs frees us from having to make decisions or feel the burden of them.

The conscious use of any substance, legal or illegal it may be, should be respected and included in the path of life of those who choose it. What can't be tolerated is the fact that others can decide how your mind, your biochemistry, your sleep-wake rhythms should operate.

I have written elsewhere (BUCALO G. 1996b) that the refusal to take psychotropic drugs by the vast majority of psychiatric patients, does not come from their *lack of insight into their illness*, let alone from their fear of physical harm they cause. There is not even an a priori refusal of substances that alter one's state of consciousness (if it is true that those who hear *voices* often use alcohol or drugs to try and contain this experience). The fundamental reason for this strenuous opposition to psychiatric *treatment* is, in my opinion, a rejection of the ideology in which the prescription of psychotropic drugs is included. Between the serenase prescribed by the specialist and the serenase taken and managed by Emy after 1 year, there is an unbridgeable distance. The former was a drug that, by the mere fact of taking it, presupposed the acceptance of the unreality of her perceptions and experiences. The latter became a tool, the only one at her disposal to her knowledge, to enforce a break in the *siege* of the voices. It was no coincidence that the chemical effects of the substance appeared and were substantially different.

When you self-prescribe a substance, it is not a denial of your own experience; you beat a strategic retreat in the face of an enemy that you recognize as real, but that you are aware of not being able to deal with. When the same substance is prescribed by others, it is an imposition of an unconditional surrender to an enemy that no one recognizes as such.

Romme cites psychiatric studies which state that about 1/3 of the people who *hear voices* and take medications, do not experience any benefit. For the other 2/3 is possible to envisage the effect of devitalisation described by Emy. One no longer has the energy to articulate a living relationship with one's own existence and one's own perceptions. As well as, occasionally, the *apparent* disappearance of the voices.

Even in those experiences where people testify to the *positive* effect of the drugs on the perception of voices, these nullify them. The self-definition that people give of being *ill* is not the realization of an objective fact, but a *strategy* itself to cope with the voices.

The book by Lori SHILLER, even though it is sponsored by the pharmaceutical industry, is an example of this. Lori writes:

"From time to time I still hear the Voices but I try to follow my own advice: I distract myself, I tell myself off, I focus on the outside world. I taught myself to use a little trick when they reappear: "These voices are not real, don't panic, don't get nervous, they are not real, don't allow them to take the upper hand, try to think of what happened before you heard them. Is there any emotion you can identify which helps explain why they are here now? They're not real, it's okay, don't be afraid".

When I hear the Voices, I shake myself and go back to reality using all of my senses. If I am on the train to Manhattan, for example, I focus on the taste of Diet Coke and the smell of my perfume. I look out the window at the changing landscape and I listen carefully to the sound of the inspector that collects the tickets. I feel my ticket that moves back and forth between my fingers." (SHILLER L. 1994, pp. 312-313)

There are no right or wrong *strategies*, each person finds their own one that most suits their needs and sensitivity. We can disagree with the emphasis with which Lori talks about the drug that changed her relationship with the voices, just like someone else will not find Eillen's reliance on the divine will *liberating*. It's impossible, after all, to define *who* the people that can be considered *free* are. And then again, free *from what*?

It's very likely that a prolonged use of psychotropic drugs leads to an inability to perceive the *voices*. But putting a lead on this phenomenon, besides being inhumane and unnecessary, in the long run will cause social, personal and health damage that are often irreversible (tardive dyskinesia, isolation, social exclusion, internment ...).

Lori herself grasps the issue when she concludes

"For years I tried to hide the Voices because I assumed people were afraid of them, but lately I've found that this is not always the case.

When one of the mail carriers that make distribution in our building appeared intrigued, I gave him an article about me and my story. He was young and I watched him carefully as he read it. Eventually he looked up.

"Do you hear voices?" he asked incredulously.

"Yes, it happens to me sometimes" I said, and waited for a look of horror to appear on his face.

But his look was instead of pure admiration.

"Wow!" he said, with incredible enthusiasm.

I wanted to hug him". (SHILLER L. 1994, pag. 313)

Experiences such as *hearing voices* are complex and dynamic phenomena. No strategy or substance can control permanently its evolution. What we have before us is not a pathological process, or a specific thing: we are faced with a meaningful relationship between human (or not) beings with the emotions, doubts, desires, contradictions that belong to it. There is a story that must be modelled every day, which must be faced and which should be given a meaning every day. It can be useful, at times, to numb ourselves and sleep, to become so insensitive as to not be touched, to lose self-awareness, but under no circumstances this may be imposed on us or may become a way of life.

The *voices* are very clear on this. JAYNES writes:

"A paranoid patient saw the word poison appearing in the air at the very moment when the nurse made him take the medication." (JAYNES J. 1984, p. 121)

Not always the truth is recognised as such. Often psychiatry calls it *paranoia* and we pretend not to hear.

EPILOGUE

Don Juan said that the humane alternatives are all that we, as people, are able to choose. They refer to the level of our daily range of action, the known, and are therefore quite limited in number and scope. Human possibilities, on the other hand, belong to the unknown. They are not what we are able to choose as people, but what we are able to achieve as human beings.

(C. CASTANEDA)

I hope I have been able to show that *hearing voices* can be sensibly regarded as a *human possibility*, inscribed in our genetic and cultural heritage. Hence as something that we should learn to know rather than fearing it, to manage rather than denying it.

Although psychiatry confirms our assumption that we have no accountability nor role in determining this experience, the fact is that we are not dealing with a *process*, but a *relationship*. This means that the evolution and the nature of the relationship between the *hearer* and the *voice* are not determined biochemically, but are influenced, socially and psychologically, by the personality of both, their sensitivity, their desires ... and last but not least, by the human environment in which this relationship of theirs takes place.

In other words, although we are allowed to have doubts about the *objective* existence of the *voices*, we can't deny the existence of a *relationship* with them. The examples of dialogue shown in these pages seem to show that.

In order for an experience to be *real*, or to produce effects *on* reality, for that matter, it is sufficient that it is considered as such by the person who experiences it. It's a bit like the story of psychiatry that affects the physical and psychological *reality* of millions of people, based on an idea of which it has never shown the *objective* existence. *Mental illness* is considered a fact that is so *obvious* and *real* that it convinces us to invest significant resources to build healthcare facilities, to experiment treatments, to train staff... but it, as shown more than sensibly by Thomas SZASZ, scientifically *does not exist.*

The definition *mental illness* does not mean anything existing in nature, either inside or outside of us; it is a faith or a belief that responds to collective needs to impose control on experiences that are beyond our social and mental order. Our faith in *mental illness* is not dissimilar in substance from the belief of some people in the divine origin of lightning, tides, solar eclipses and other visible events. It is born from the same ignorance and fear itself.

The question of the *objective* existence of the voices, then, maybe is a false problem. But, as above, whether it is so or not, it captivates us, it causes distress to us and it requires a response. The fact that we can feel the problem that arises is unreal, does not change the urgency of having to solve it, or the fear of making mistakes. If a person does not leave his house because he *hears* someone in the street that threatens to kill him, we can conclude that he is wrong because we can't *hear*, or *see* anyone in the street, but we should never deny his terror. It is neither meaningful nor human; least of all this attitude can be called help or, even worse, therapy.

But let's try to face the issue.

Each *voice* has individual and, therefore, unique and unrepeatable identity, character and goals. It's probably incorrect to classify them by categories, but we need to be able to orient ourselves in a world in which our rational capacities and our understanding of reality are not worth much.

I do not like classifications that divide the voices into good and bad, male and female, from above and from below... These ratings and comments are part of the rapport and the history of the relationship of each person with their own *voices*. What seems to me more fundamental to the understanding of this experience is on one hand defining their nature, on the other hand their *ways* of communication. In other words, it's about defining *who* and *what* they are and *where from* they speak.

The key distinction about their nature is whether they are *embodied* or *disembodied* voices. The former have an earthly body and are generally known, living or not, persons. The latter are spiritual and unknown demonic or divine beings. Both of them can speak from *inside* or *outside* our head. This distinction is crucial in order to understand the kind of influence and power that they can exert on us, but also to properly address the question of the *evidence* of their existence.

But let's proceed in an orderly fashion.

In the case of disembodied and unknown *voices*, the problem of their objective existence defies every scientific solution. If the *voice* tells us and shows us that it is God or some other supernatural entity, the inability to prove its *objectivity* is proof itself, of its *reality*. The relationship between man and gods, after all, has always been of an individual nature, and invisible to most people. If we browse the sacred texts, in fact, it is difficult to find a collective revelation of the divine truth. The *voice* of God always chooses and speaks to *someone*, the chosen one, who then has a lot to do to show others the divine nature of the message he/she conveys.

If at one time, just like Teresa of Avila, they had to defend themselves from the charge of being an instrument of the devil, nowadays, nonetheless, they must prove their sanity if they want to avoid being sectioned in a psychiatric institution. When Christ told his disciples that they would have been persecuted for speaking *in his name*, he was stating, in my opinion, the basic truth that following one's inner *voice* leads to an inevitable clash with the order of shared reality.

What *evidence* can a person bring to prove he was really *chosen* by God? If we analyze our own collective unconscious, we can easily find the answer. It's the same *evidence* that God gives to the person to prove his existence and his choice: the *miracle*. With it the *voice* of God acts directly in the world of material reality, transforming it and showing its *objectivity* as a force that is able to change it. The miracle is used both to designate the chosen person (the stigmata produced on the body of Francis of Assisi are of this nature), and to prove the person's credibility in the eyes of the human community in which the person is included (for example, the multiplication of the loaves and fishes or the walk of Jesus on top of the water are of this nature).

In any case the *miracles* are observable realities that transcend and escape the natural laws that, we believe, dominate our lives. The *miracle* turns around, in other words, the relationship between body and soul, showing that it is the latter to give life and to make the former possible. The famous saying of Mohammed and the mountain clarifies the concept even better: what we believe determines what it *is*. The formula that Jesus used to explain the miracles is symptomatic; it is not him, but our faith that changes us. If you think about it, that's the way it is.

But if it is indeed impossible to escape from the paradox of knowledge that we experience when we *hear* the voice of supernatural – and, therefore imperceptible - beings, a different matter is the experience of *hearing the voices* of embodied people, who are known to us and perceived by us also in *shared* reality. I'm talking about living people, as the perception of deceased persons who are known to us implies different e*vidence* and cultural contexts of reference (the spiritualist philosophy and science that we talked about in the prologue).

How can the person Emy hears talk to her, for example? And how can Emy hear it? Her answer seems sensible: it's a matter of *telepathy*. But how can she *prove* it, especially if it is not confirmed by the people who are in contact with her? None of them admits talking to her, or that they had ever thought about the things she says she has *heard* from them. And then one of two different paths is undertaken: either their silence is detected as a conspiracy to make us mad; or one can believe, as does Emy, this broadcasting may be unconscious.

The *voices*, in fact, seem to be of the same kind of the sensible sounds emitted by our larynx and, at the same time, to have the same immateriality and inaudibility of our thoughts. They do not respond only to what we say but also to our intentions, to what we think, to what we want. Somehow we seem to *hear* with our ears our thoughts or the thoughts of others, as if something had amplified them to the point of losing control over them.

The fact that language can make a selection and mediation of what we think, allowing us to just say what we want or can say at any given time, allows us to have some control over our relationships. It is everybody's common experience that if we *always* said everything we thought, we would be left with very little of the sensible and relational life that we have. In order to be able to live in this as in any other reality we have to compromise with our instincts and our minds. In all this, there is not any conflict between thoughts and feelings as both are uncontrollable. What we can control, to some extent, and with more or less success, is their expression. In optimal situations we can bring *out* (or have the illusion of doing so) only what we believe is in line with the image that we have built of us or with the expectations that we think others have of us.

This delicate balance between *inside* and *outside*, *self* and *others* is based partly on language. Let me give you an example. In communicating our inner experiences, normally we use a series of mediations that we call *common sense* or *good manners*. We almost never say it like it is: generally we say it like we believe or like we were taught they should be said. This mediation becomes a selection of which of our thoughts and our experiences are socialisable and, therefore, viable and which are, instead, to be considered aberrations or perversions of our mind.

In other words, everything that happens (or seems to happen) *within* us, we can only accept a small part. What about all the *rest* of it? Psychoanalytic theory suggests that this *waste*, which is often far superior to what passes in our social life, is collected gradually in a *place* of our psyche called unconscious, where it is organized and structured like a parallel personality, putting together the *scraps* of our thoughts, our emotions and desires. This *unconscious* personality shares the same physical space of ours, but it has a story and maybe even a *voice* that are different from ours. It doesn't have a body and it can exist only through us, only through our eyes it can see and it can hear only through our ears.

I do not know if there is anywhere anything that looks like the unconscious that Freud imagined. But surely it has nothing to do with that kind of inventory of removed and disposed *things* that the Freudian theory describes. The *waste* we are looking for consists of experiences, emotions, *living* sensations. It is neither the photos of what we were nor the memory of what we were doing; but it is everything that we could have been and that we have never been. It is not things but an*other* we that was never born, who has never become incarnate but who *has* *existed* and *exists*, unseen and unheard *inside* but also *outside* of us.

It may be that this *other* of ours talks with Emy, as much as it's possible that her *other* talks to her. In any case Emy does not speak *to herself*, like her appearance and our fear would have us believe. Maybe she does not even speak with us as we know us; nevertheless that which she feels pertains us, in the same way that the memories that others have of us pertain us. We are no longer those that others remember, but at the same time we are: we can refuse to recognize ourselves in their memories, but we can't say that we have nothing to do with it. We *are* those memories too, for better or worse.

Of course this does not *prove* anything, even if we are paradoxically able to consider *delirious* those who say that we are in telepathic contact with them, while we consider *real*, to the point of paying good money for it, that someone explains to us that our refusal to serve in the military stems from the unresolved conflict with our father about the carnal knowledge of our mother.

In fact, most of the *obvious* theories and explanations that justify our actions and understand those of others come from experiences, intuitions, phenomena that can't be *explained* or *proven*. Those who believe in God, for example, *know* that he exists, although up till now they would not be able to bring a single scientific *proof* of his existence. Similarly, theories like the Jungian one, as C. JUNG confirms in his autobiography, arise from hallucinatory experiences that showed him, in the reality of his existence, what he then theorized as the eruption of the *collective unconscious* in the individual history of each person. (see. C.G.JUNG 1984)

JUNG writes, with regards to his experiences of dialogue with the *voices*:

"I was bringing with me thoughts about which I could not talk

to anyone; they would have just been misunderstood. I felt in the most painful way the gap between the outside world and my inner world: neither could I grasp yet the interaction between these two worlds that I clearly see today. (...)

However, from the outset it was clear to me that I could have a relationship with the outside world and with people, only if I could show, and this would have required the utmost care, that the content of mental experiences is **real***, and not just as my own experiences, but as collective experiences that others may also have. Later, I tried to show this in my scientific work, but before that I did everything in my power to communicate a new perspective to those who were close to me. I knew if I had failed to do that I would have been condemned to absolute aloneness."* (JUNG C.G. 1984, p. 239)

If we wanted to take this passage of JUNG to the extreme, we could say that Jung's theory is nothing but the attempt of a man to not be considered *crazy*. Certainly a successful attempt, which not only confirms the fact that the *voices* are a *modality* of consciousness of reality, but also that it is a vital imperative for those who *hear* them to show to those who are close to them the *reality* of their experience. There is no other way to escape the *absolute aloneness* mentioned by Jung. It reigns supreme both when we try to keep the *voices* for ourselves, and in the even more frequent case when others do not believe that our experience is everybody's assets.

Incidentally, the strategy used by Jung to contain this *invasion* of his life by the collective unconscious, is described as being anchored by things and people of his life in the *shared* reality.

"It was very important for me to have a normal life in the real world, to balance the strangeness of the inner world. My family and my profession continued to be the ground to which I could always go back to in order to regain the security of being an actually existing common man. (...)

They would prove to me daily that I really existed, that I was not a leaf swaying to the winds of the spirit, like Nietzsche. He had let the ground fail beneath his feet because he had nothing but the inner world of his thoughts (and, moreover, he was pretty possessed by them). He had no roots anymore, and hovered above the earth, and therefore had collapsed into exaggeration and unreality. For me, such an unreality was the quintessential horror, as my purpose was, after all, in this *world and in* this *life.* " (JUNG C.G. 1984, p. 233)

That is without denying the value of his experience, but trying not to be overwhelmed by it.

If we accept the premise that the content of Jung's mental experiences are *real*, we can solve the problem that afflicts us without further casualties. Let's not forget, however, that the experience of the *voices* is located in a border area between the world of perception and that of thought. Between the world that is subject to partly known physical laws and the one that follows the unfathomable laws of the human psyche. The *evidence* that we use to confirm the accuracy of a perception or that which seems essential to verify the meaningfulness of a thought, don't serve any purpose in this area.

The *voices* are not audible sounds, but they are not a creation of the psyche either. If treating them as pathological symptoms or misperceptions lead to devastating results in the lives of those who hear them, considering them an expression of the imagination, desires or psychological complexes of an individual, can be just as harmful and useless. Psychology and psychiatry, in this, share the same purpose: to control the experience of people, depriving them of the opportunity to explain it themselves and communicate its content. Between *symbolic* and *hallucinatory* experience there is indeed little difference: we *believe we hear voices*, but we *really* don't.

The hypothesis of JUNG, which we now know was born from the

need to find a personal frame of reference for his *voices*, is, perhaps, the exception that proves the rule. *Voices* exist and some of us are able to perceive them. They are not the *result* of either our biochemistry, or our psychodynamics; psyche and biochemistry contribute only to make it possible to hear them. JUNG believed that some of these communications come from the heritage of the collective experiences of our species, somehow inscribed in our genes. A remarkable convergence with what JAYNES said about the fact that the voices of the gods who led the men to take root on our planet are *recorded* in the right hemisphere, where their *memory* and meaning are preserved.

Given certain physical and psychological situations, the channel of communication between collective subconscious (right hemisphere) and aware ego (left hemisphere) is reactivated. This seems to occur either spontaneously (e.g. when an event of extraordinary emotional impact disrupts the rational control of our mind) or through specific techniques developed by all the mystical, magical or hallucinogenic cultural traditions.

The experience in these two cases takes place in a very different way.

In the first case, what is released and passes through us is largely related to our past and present individual history. The *voices* we hear are those of our loved ones or friends, who can console us or blame us for what happened. Often this experience disorients us, increasingly confusing the boundaries between our thoughts and the thoughts of others', and, above all, between the *voices* that we only can hear and those that are shared with others. It is not uncommon in this situation to expose ourselves in situations where we appear inconsistent, strange or bizarre.

This experience exposes itself to psychological interpretation precisely because of its capacity to dramatize our human and relational history. In fact, the *voices* we hear sink their claws on the unresolved wounds, the doubts, the fears we have, exposing us to terror and ridicule.

Treating it *only* from the psychological point of view, as a mere manifestation of our inner needs, does not do justice to the complexity of the experience that we are living. After all, it is not clear if the *voices* are born *from* our conflicts or, on the contrary, they use them and point them out to achieve their goal: controlling the mind that hosts them.

In the second case, that of voluntary techniques to access altered states of consciousness and perception, the path is completely different. Here we expect that a *voice* or a *guide* emerges, ready to get down to listening and equipped with cultural tools to catalog, define and use the knowledge that derives from this experience.

In this case, the psychological and individual element is just the motivation that drives the individual to explore his/her possibilities and to face the unknown. What emerges from this experience can hardly be forced into the frameworks of our (so-called) *human* sciences: this is in fact something *objective* and *universal*, which constitutes us as we are.

Our attempt of *psychologizing* these experiences (whether they are voluntary or involuntary) has nothing to do with the need to understand *what* or *who* is invading our mental order. In fact, the psychological interpretation tends to lock the issue *into* us by replacing the lively *dialogue* with the *voices* with a senseless and crazy inner *monologue*.

For that matter, the *voices* are part of our mental life by default; they enter in the order of our thoughts and often share with us the space of our body. The *voices* have desires, they have memory; they misunderstand and are misunderstood... they have their own psychological structure that often has nothing to do with our culture and personality. They are not the mere expression of something, just like we are not the simple emanation of our parents. Even if we assume that they are born *from* us, this does not allow us to reduce them to the way our senses or our biochemistry work.

Similarly, it is illogical to think of getting to the bottom of it by acting on our mind or our psychology, just like it makes no sense that anyone would think of making us stop talking by shutting our parents' mouths. Once they are *brought to life*, the *voices*, just like for example the ideas expressed in this book, do not belong to us anymore.

The hearers who attempt to evade the various psychiatric therapies that promise to free them from their *voices*, clearly know this elementary truth. They know that everything that will be done by psychiatrists will be done *to them*. So the medications, seclusion, engagement in forced social situations, the diagnosis of insanity... The idea that the purpose of the *voices* can be to drive us crazy is the result of a perverse convergence between them and our therapists. In fact, nothing is usually done to stop the *voices* invading our lives. Paradoxically, all psychiatric therapies tend to weaken and limit *our* ability to perceive: this is like saying that, in front of someone who threatens us, instead of running away or dealing with it in order to understand and resolve the issue, we plug our ears so we can't hear it. That's all very well. We can argue about the futility of this choice, but we can't disrespect it. Except that this hearing loss is imposed on us by those who believe that no one is threatening us and, therefore, there is no one to protect. Not only that, the effect psychiatric therapies (especially the psychopharmacological ones) have on our perception and consciousness, are much broader and deeper than a temporary deafness to the voices, if only because there is no substance that can act selectively *just* on a few ideas , thoughts, actions or perceptions. You can't become *deaf* to the voices and think that you can continue to hear yourself and others with clarity, depth and participation. It's as if I kicked the radio that turns on in the morning to wake me up, and then I tried to listen to my favorite song.

Prior to radically affecting our biochemistry, we should be very sure that there is no better way to understand, modify, or manage our perceptions. On the contrary, psychiatric therapy sees this chemical invasion as the elective way to intervene. You may say that some have found benefit in this energetic approach on our senses. Many of the psychiatric patients deny, after treatment or hospitalization, that they *hear voices*. The majority of them are forced to lie. The perverse logic that prevails in psychiatry considers every treatment *failure* as a resistance on the part of the person or of the *illness*, and never as an inadequacy of the treatment. People *must* be mentally ill, they *must* feel as such, they *must* find benefit from therapies that affect their brain; it is only this way that psychiatry can claim for itself the status of medical science. The senseless fury with which these doctors have operated on the brains of their patients, without any acknowledgment or *evidence* of the correctness of their hypothesis can't be otherwise explained.

Besides this official version that is imposed by psychiatry, reflections and research have grown in recent years, first on a personal level and then collectively, by the voice *hearers* that agree with some of the ideas that are described in this book:

- *hearing voices* is not an illness, but a *modality* and a *possibility* of human perception;
- this perceptual experience, like any other experience that concerns our senses and our sensibilities, is not to be *treated* or changed a priori, but *understood* and *managed*;
- it is necessary to have a *dialogue* with the voices: to ignore them or try to distract yourself is not useful;
- the *management* of this *dialogue* comes from recognising it as such and openly and clearly confronting

the *voices* about their identity and possible mutual influences;

- the *voices* exist, but that doesn't mean that they are always right;
- the *voices* relate to us, but that doesn't mean that they are our fantasies or that they necessarily care for us;
- we are not alone *hearing them*: hearing voices is a real and universal experience;
- it is necessary to know and get in touch with other *voice hearers*: *only* those who go through or have gone through this experience can help.

The path that I have tried to show in these pages is, as the Buddhists say, just *a finger pointing at the moon*. There are so many other pointed fingers, personal paths and experiences that are excluded or are destroyed in this unnecessary and inhumane attempt to silence the *voices* that speak to us.

As it was the case for other experiences, it is necessary that the *voice hearers* get out of the emotional and social ghetto in which we have locked them up, to return to invade our daily lives and order. Only a collective movement, built on the stories of *real* relationship with the voices, can restart our search for our meaning of being human.

A shared experience collectively recognised as such, escapes the suffocating control of psychiatry, and returns to be human *possibility*. A *possibility* that is still essential for us to get where we are unable to get and understand reality in its truth.

This *handbook* is an invitation to those who hear and those who can't hear the voices to break the silence, to get organized and beat a *common* path. After all, the Buddhist wisdom reminds us that no matter if you look or you keep your eyes closed, things are what they are. We are not talking about two different worlds, then, we look at and feel the world from two different angles. The *invisible* air is as essential to our lives as the visible food we swallow; as well as the *inaudible* passage of blood through our veins is as a part of reality as the sound of the water flowing in a stream.

The experience of *dialogue* with the voices is a journey through reality; we all have to make it *possible*. I have tried to show how those who do not hear voices can help those who hear them and they can let those who hear voices help them understand.

There is no one and only prescribed path. The only indication that should guide us is given by Don Juan:

> *"For me there is only one way, the one along paths that have a heart, along any path that has a heart. Along this I walk; and the only evidence that counts is the going through it in its full length. And here I walk while I'm looking, and looking, breathless."*

(C. CASTANEDA, 1970)

BIBLIOGRAPHY

1. ANTONUCCI G. (1989), *Il pregiudizio psichiatrico*, Eleuthera [*The Psychiatric Prejudice*]

2. ANTONUCCI G. (1993), *Critica al giudizio psichiatrico*, Sensibili alle foglie [*A Critique To The Psychiatric Judgement*]

3. ANTONUCCI G., COPPOLA A. (1995), *Il telefono viola contro i metodi della psichiatria*, Eleuthera [*The Purple Hotline Against Psychiatric Methods*]

4. BREGGIN P. (1984), *Elettroshock. I guasti del cervello*, Feltrinelli [Breggin, Peter R. *Electroshock: Its Brain-Disabling Effects* (1979). New York: Springer Publishing Company]

5. BREGGIN P. (1985), *A brief history of psychiatry*, Phoenix Rising, vol. 5, no. 2/3

6. BUCALO G. (1993), *Dietro ogni scemo c'è un villaggio. Itinerari per fare a meno della psichiatria*, Sicilia Punto L [*Behind Every Fool There Is A Village. Itineraries Without Psychiatry*]

7. BUCALO G. (1994), *Psicologia, comunità, differenza*, in AA.VV., *Porolano di psicologia*, Centro di documentazione [*Psychology, Community, Diversity*, in VV.AA., *Pilot Book of Psychology*]

8. BUCALO G. (1996a), *La malattia mentale non esiste. Antipsichiatria: prime istruzioni d'uso*, Nautilus [Bucalo G., *Mental illness does not exist. Antipsychiatry – Basic Operating Instructions*, (2014). Amazon]

9. BUCALO G. (1996b), *Malati di niente. Manuale minimo di sopravvivenza psichiatrica*, Calusca Grafton [*Nullatics. Psychiatric Survival Basic Handbook*]

10. CADDY E. (1993), *Il mio volo verso la libertà*, Amrita [*Flight into freedom* (1988, with Liza Hollingshead), Published by Element]

11. CARCANO M. (1995), *Utero astrale*, Filema [*Astral Womb*]

12. CASTANEDA C. (1970), *A scuola dallo stregone*, Astrolabio [*The Teachings of Don Juan: A Yaqui Way of Knowledge* (1968)]

13. CASTANEDA C. (1992), *Il fuoco dal profondo*, Rizzoli [*The Fire From Within* (1984)]

14. CESTARI R. (1994), *L'inganno psichiatrico*, Sensibili alle foglie [The Psychiatric Scam]

15. CHAMBERLIN J. (1990), *Da noi stessi. Un contributo per l'auto-aiuto psichiatrico*, Primerano [*On Our Own: Patient Controlled Alternatives to the Mental Health System*. New York: Haworth Press, 1978]

16. COOPER D. (1977), *Grammatica del vivere*, Feltrinelli [*Grammar of Living*, Penguin, 1974]

17. COOPER D. (1978), *Psichiatria e antipsichiatria*, Armando [*Psychiatry and Anti-Psychiatry*, Paladin (1967)]

18. COOPER D. (1979), *Il linguaggio della follia*, Feltrinelli [*The Language of Madness*, Penguin. 1978]

19. CURCIO R., VALENTINO N., PETRELLI S. (1990), *Nel bosco di Bistorco*, Sensibili alle foglie [The Woods of Bistorco]

20. ELIADE M. (1988), *Lo sciamanismo*, Ed. Mediterranee [*Shamanism: Arcaic Techniques of Ecstasy*, first published in 1951]

21. ERIKSON E.H. (1974), *Gioventù e crisi di identità*, Armando [*Identity: Youth and Crisis,* 1968]

22. FORTI L. (1979), a cura di, *L'altra pazzia*, Feltrinelli [*The Other Madness*, ed. by Laura Forti]

23. GIOVETTI P. (1990), *Findhorn*, Ed. Mediterranee

24. GROF S. (1990), *Oltre il cervello*, Cittadella [*Beyond the Brain: Birth, Death And Transcendence In Psychotherapy* (1985)]

25. GROF S. e C. (1993), a cura di, *Emergenza spirituale*, RED [*Spiritual Emergency: When Personal Transformation Becomes A Crisis* (1989), Edited with Christina Grof]

26. HOFMANN A. (1995), *LSD. Il mio bambino difficile.* Urra-Apogeo [*LSD — My Problem Child*, McGraw-Hill Book Company, 1980]

27. HUXLEY A. (1992), *Le porte della percezione*, Mondadori [*The Doors of Perception*, 1954]

28. JAYNES J. (1984), *Il crollo della mente bicamerale e l'origine della coscienza*, Adelphi [*The Origin of Consciousness in the Breakdown of the Bicameral* Mind (1976)]

29. JUNG C.G. (1984), *Ricordi, sogni, riflessioni*, Rizzoli [Jung, C. G., & Jaffe A. (1962). *Memories, Dreams, Reflections*. London: Collins. This is Jung's autobiography, recorded and edited by Aniela Jaffe]

30. LAING R.D. (1978), *I fatti della vita*, Einaudi [*The Facts of Life*. Penguin. 1976]

31. LAING R.D. (1979a), *Al di là della psichiatria*, Newton Compton [Laing, Ronald David, *The Man and His Ideas*, 1976]

32. LAING R.D. (1979b), *Intervista sul folle e il saggio*, Laterza [*Interview on The Madman and The Wiseman*, by Vincenzo Caretti, 1979, Laterza]

33. LAING R.D. (1980), *La politica dell'esperienza*, Feltrinelli [*The Politics of Experience and the Bird of Paradise*, 1967, Penguin]

34. LAING R.D. (1982), *La nascita dell'esperienza*, Mondadori [*The Voice of Experience: Experience, Science and Psychiatry*, 1982]

35. LAPASSADE G. (1980), *Saggio sulla transe*, Feltrinelli [*Essay on Trance*]

36. LAPASSADE G. (1993), *Stati modificati e transe*, Sensibili alle foglie [*Altered States and Trance*]

37. LAPASSADE G. (1996), *Transe e dissociazione*, Sensibili alle foglie [*Trance and Dissociation*]

38. PETACCO A. (1978), *Il Cristo dell'Amiata*, Mondadori [*The Christ of Amiata*]

39. ROMME M.A.J., ESCHER A.D.M.A.C. (1988), *Hearing voices*, in AA.VV., *Research in community psichiatry*, Van Gorcum

40. SCHATZMAN M. (1980), *Storia di Ruth*, Feltrinelli [*The Story of Ruth*]

41. SHILLER L. (1995), *La stanza del silenzio*, NIS [*The Quiet Room*]

42. SUZUKI D.T. (1975), *Saggi sul buddismo zen*, Ed. Mediterranee [*essays in Zen Buddhism*]

43. SZASZ T. (1966), *Il mito della malattia mentale*, Il Saggiatore [*The Myth of Mental Illness*, 1961]

44. SZASZ T. (1977), *Disumanizzazione dell'uomo*, Feltrinelli [*Ideology and Insanity: Essays on the Psychiatric Dehumanization of Man*, 1970]

45. SZASZ T. (1979), *Schizofrenia. Simbolo sacro della psichiatria*, Armando [*Schizophrenia: The Sacred Symbol of Psychiatry*, 1976]

46. SZASZ T. (1981), *Il mito della psicoterapia*, Feltrinelli [*The Myth of Psychotherapy: Mental Healing as Religion, Rhetoric, and Repression*, 1978]

47. TART C. (1977), *Stati di coscienza*, Astrolabio [*States of Consciousness*, 1975]

48. TERESA di GESU' (1985), *Opere*, Postulazione Generale OCD [*Works of Teresa of Avila*]

49. ZOLLA E. (1992), *Uscite dal mondo*, Adelphi [Out of this World]

50. ZOLLA E. (1994), *Lo stupore infantile*, Adelphi [The Wonder of Childhood]

www.ingramcontent.com/pod-product-compliance
Lightning Source LLC
Chambersburg PA
CBHW062010280526
45787CB00005B/2046